ALA Editions • **SPECIAL REPORTS**

A LIBRARIAN'S GUIDE TO
AN UNCERTAIN JOB MARKET

JEANNETTE WOODWARD

AMERICAN LIBRARY ASSOCIATION
Chicago   2011

Jeannette Woodward is a principal of Wind River Library and Nonprofit Consulting. After a career in academic library administration, she began a second career in public libraries as the director of the Fremont County Library System in Wyoming. Woodward is the author of several books, the most recent of which include *Countdown to a New Library,* 2nd edition (ALA, 2010) and *The Customer-Driven Academic Library* (ALA, 2008). Woodward holds a master's degree in library and information science from Rutgers University with doctoral study at the University of Texas at Austin.

© 2011 by the American Library Association. Any claim of copyright is subject to applicable limitations and exceptions, such as rights of fair use and library copying pursuant to Sections 107 and 108 of the U.S. Copyright Act. No copyright is claimed in content that is in the public domain, such as works of the U.S. government.

Printed in the United States of America

15 14 13 12 11   5 4 3 2 1

While extensive effort has gone into ensuring the reliability of the information in this book, the publisher makes no warranty, express or implied, with respect to the material contained herein.

ISBNs: 978-0-8389-1105-1 (paper); 978-0-8389-9298-2 (PDF); 978-0-8389-9299-9 (ePub); 978-0-8389-9300-2 (Mobipocket); 978-0-8389-9301-9 (Kindle). For more information on digital formats, visit the ALA Store at alastore.ala.org and select eEditions.

Library of Congress Cataloging-in-Publication Data

Woodward, Jeannette A.
   A librarian's guide to an uncertain job market / Jeannette Woodward.
      p. cm.
   Includes bibliographical references and index.
   ISBN 978-0-8389-1105-1 (alk. paper)
   1. Library science—Vocational guidance—United States. 2. Librarians—Employment—United States. I. Title.
   Z682.35.V62W66 2011
   020'.2373—dc22   2011011672

Series cover design by Casey Bayer.
Series text design in Palatino Linotype and Avenir by Karen Sheets de Gracia.

♾ This paper meets the requirements of ANSI/NISO Z39.48–1992 (Permanence of Paper).

*To my family,
Chris, Laura, Lowell,
John, and Davey,
with all my love.*

ALA Editions purchases fund advocacy, awareness, and accreditation programs for library professionals worldwide.

CONTENTS

Introduction vii

1 Employment Prospects for LIS Professionals 1

2 Hoping for the Best: Recession-Proofing Your Present Job 13

3 Preparing for the Worst: Sensible Precautions for Unsettled Times 21

4 When the Ax Falls: First Aid for Dealing with Sudden Job Loss 29

5 Step by Step: A Job-Hunting Primer 35

6 Changing Directions: When It's Time to Move On 47

7 First Impressions: Applications that Make the Cut 57

8 Composing the Well-Tempered Résumé 67

9 Surviving and Triumphing: Secrets of Successful Interviews 81

Index 95

INTRODUCTION

Library and information science professionals have long been accustomed to providing a wealth of job-hunting materials to patrons who have lost their jobs. In fact, we are perhaps the best source of free career guidance in our communities. However, the "great recession," as it is being called, has brought the topic of job loss much closer to home. Government agencies—the employers of most librarians—are experiencing huge budget deficits, and corporate employers are looking at every position that might be a candidate for elimination. Of course, all LIS professionals must occasionally go through the ordeal of finding a new job and most of us have lost a job at least once during the course of our careers. However, as a profession, we have not experienced so many layoffs since the Great Depression.

ECONOMIC AND DEMOGRAPHIC PROSPECTS

In one sense, we should feel grateful that LIS has not seen a catastrophic decline like some occupations. Studies indicate that the average librarian is a woman in her 50s and many are in their 60s. Because we are in the unusual situation of having many retirees and soon-to-become retirees among our numbers, libraries continue to have openings for new graduates. More experienced librarians may be feeling nothing more than a little anxiety.

Unfortunately, that is not the case in libraries where repeated waves of budget cuts have resulted in crisis situations where drastic measures are necessary. At first, perhaps the library or its parent institution made retirement a little more attractive with modest severance packages. About that same time, new hires were frozen, substitute and temporary staff were cut, and part-time hours were reduced. As the budget crisis continued, full-time staff were forced to take unpaid leave (furloughs) and eventually every small cache of nonessential spending was exhausted. Because the current recession began in 2008, libraries may be on their second or third round of cuts. Layoffs have become more common and many LIS professionals may be experiencing reductions in benefits, hours, and salaries. Others live in a constant state of anxiety because they don't know whether their jobs are secure and interpret every rumor as evidence that they may soon be out of work.

Job Holders and Job Seekers

This book is intended for librarians and other LIS professionals whose situations are somewhere on that continuum from job anxiety to actual job loss. It will describe effective ways to make your job as recession-proof as possible and to prepare for whatever slings and arrows outrageous fortune (in the form of your local government, school district, university, or corporation) is sending your way. It is not at all paranoid to take precautions now even if your job is in no immediate danger. The axe has already fallen for some readers, so the book also focuses on surviving a period of unemployment both financially and emotionally while taking effective steps to make it as brief as possible.

As you have discovered, this book is quite brief and cannot answer all your questions nor provide guidance for every situation. However, our libraries are bursting with books and articles about job hunting, résumé writing, interviews, and other information needed by our patrons. Most of those sources will be relevant to your situation, but as we all know, our profession is a world of its own. This book is therefore intended to fill in some of the gaps and add the experiences of many LIS job seekers to your rapidly expanding store of knowledge.

Our libraries' career resources are just one example of the many advantages that LIS professionals have over job applicants in other occupations. Perhaps even more useful than our career collections are our own personal research skills. These allow us to manage our finances more successfully, understand our rights, take advantage of the benefits to which we are entitled, and fully investigate the job openings we are considering. Although we are all individuals and our talents are varied, the kind of talents that attract us to LIS can also make us unusually effective job seekers.

Financial and Psychological Costs

Most LIS professionals are not accustomed to facing economic uncertainty. Ours has been a very stable profession and once we each acquired some relevant experience, we usually found it fairly easy to pursue our professional goals. Jobs, though not plentiful, were usually numerous enough to allow us the freedom to make choices, use our talents, and earn comfortable salaries. When you are not accustomed to an uncertain market, job hunting may be especially stressful. If you are not used to rejection, you may begin doubting yourself and your abilities. For this reason, it is important to know that you are not alone and that many others are going through the same painful experience. Throughout this book we'll take time out to discuss what it feels like to be unemployed and the steps you can take to preserve your optimism and protect your own mental health. In the end, most of you will retain your existing jobs or experience only a brief period of unemployment before you find new jobs. Although painful, this can be a period of increased self-awareness and growth as LIS professionals. It is not the end of the world; in fact, in some ways it may be just the beginning.

1

EMPLOYMENT PROSPECTS FOR LIS PROFESSIONALS

To make any sort of reasonably accurate estimate of the number of jobs that have been lost as a result of the recession, we must first answer some difficult questions. By the time you read this book, more information will be available. As I write, however, information from professional organizations and the media is changing so rapidly that answers must be very general and tentative. Only trends are clearly apparent; precise numbers must be considered suspect.

LIBRARIES AND THE RECESSION

When the stock market began to implode in December 2007, large corporations soon began laying off employees. Special librarians were probably the first to be personally affected by the crisis. Then the mortgage defaults that precipitated the recession created a rapid drop in real estate valuations and property taxes. Owners who bought their homes when prices were high were unable to sell for the prices they paid. Banks foreclosed on mortgages, and the glut of foreclosed properties caused the value of other homes to drop even further. Local government is largely funded by property taxes, so public libraries began feeling the crunch a year or two into the crisis.

Unlike local government, state revenues are generated by income and sales taxes. In most areas, it was perhaps a year before Main Street merchants and other smaller businesses felt the tidal wave. Their profits dropped, they paid less state income tax, and fewer customers meant lower sales tax revenues. Businesses laid off employees, who in turn paid less sales and income taxes. Colleges and universities are funded in large part by state revenue. They gradually began tightening their budgets and by perhaps the third year of the economic downturn, they were forced to take more drastic steps. State budgets consist primarily of personnel expenditures. First hiring was frozen and then staffing cuts became widespread.

Budget Cuts

The well-known subscription database vendor EBSCO surveyed libraries in February 2010 asking how current economic conditions were affecting them. The majority of those responding were academic and special libraries, but public and other library types were represented as well. Most of the individuals responding to the survey were library directors or in senior library management. Eighty-three percent reported either budget cuts or no budget growth that year. Eighty-five percent of the respondents expected additional budget cuts or flat budgets for the following year. Sixty-three percent of the respondents said that they would not fill positions that were vacant due to resignations and retirements. Fifty-seven percent said that a freeze was in place on rehires, 37 percent said they had actually eliminated positions, and 53 percent had reassigned or downgraded positions to paraprofessional or clerical status. In addition, library administrators were finding other ways to reduce staff costs, like cutting part-time hours and requiring staff to take unpaid leave.[1]

In other surveys, almost all schools reported a decrease in funding for information resources in 2009 and fewer school libraries served more students. Public libraries were serving more users and providing more services with lower budgets.

Although Wall Street began recovering quite rapidly, economists expect the job market to remain depressed for several years, and it is only after new corporate and small business hires have a chance to earn money and pay taxes, that the good news will find its way to most libraries. It can be safely assumed that only some of the positions eliminated during the crisis will ever be reinstated. Library needs are changing rapidly and new positions will gradually be created to meet these needs. However, for the next several years, job openings will depend largely upon vacancies created by retirements and other librarians leaving the profession.

Retirements

Librarians on average are older than members of other occupations. Surveys generally agree that the average librarian is a woman in her early 50s. In 2000, 2 percent of library directors were age 65 and over, the number climbing to 9 percent in 2005 and continuing to rise today. There are some differences among types of libraries, but there is no question that a large percent of the profession has reached or is nearing retirement age. How many jobs can we expect to become available as a result of retirements? Before the recession this number would have been easier to estimate, but retirements have dropped in every occupation. Librarians are fortunate in that they can more often look forward to a traditional pension. Retirees in other occupations may have only individual retirement accounts (IRAs) whose values have plummeted. However, even more stable pension plans have lost some of their value. Many librarians are looking at their options and finding that they would do well to remain in their jobs for a little longer. On the other hand, some employers are offering attractive severance packages to encourage retirements. Overall, we can probably expect somewhat more jobs opening up as a result of retirements than in other occupations.

LIS Employment Outlook

When librarians guide patrons to information about the job market, the first source they turn to is usually the U.S. government's *Occupational Outlook Handbook*. Unfortunately, the job market is changing so rapidly that the "Outlook for Librarians" section is necessarily out of date. Its conclusion that job growth will be limited by budget constraints now strikes us as the ultimate understatement. However, much of the most recent analysis is extremely relevant. For example, it says, "Jobs for librarians outside traditional settings will grow the fastest over the decade. Nontraditional librarian jobs include working as information brokers, as well as working for private corporations, nonprofit organizations, and consulting firms."[2] Of course, the employers who will hire those information brokers may need some time to get back on track financially, but there is no question that the business and professional sectors need precisely the skills that librarians possess.

The *Occupational Outlook Handbook* is even more enthusiastic about job prospects for archivists, LIS's sister profession. Although once again the relevant section of the handbook was written before the depth of the recession was fully understood, it is clear that this profession is undergoing a resurgence of vitality. Digital archives have ushered in a new and exciting era. Nevertheless, competition is expected to be keen for openings because there are a large number of qualified applicants for most positions. However, "employment of archivists, curators, and museum technicians is expected to increase 20 percent over the 2008–18 decade, which is much faster than the average for all occupations." Of course, the current slowdown will definitely affect that estimate; nevertheless, the future looks bright indeed. The section goes on to state that "demand for archivists who specialize in electronic records and records management will grow more rapidly than the demand for archivists who specialize in older media formats."[3]

Challenges Facing Libraries

Libraries are nonetheless the main employers of information professionals, and so students frequently ask which type of library offers the brightest prospects for the future. This may be the most difficult question of all to answer. Each type of library is currently experiencing major financial challenges,[4] but the great unknown is how they will emerge from economic trauma. Each type of library has endemic problems that won't completely disappear when funding becomes more plentiful. For example, declines in some usage statistics reported by academic libraries may have a long-term relationship to funding. These trends are likely to continue no matter what the state of the economy. The online availability of what have traditionally been considered library resources will play an especially important role in the future of brick-and-mortar libraries.

School libraries are also experiencing competition from online resources, but other forces are at work that are more problematic. For example, school librarians possess teaching credentials and are paid salaries similar to those of classroom teachers. Even when the economy recovers, librarians will continue to have an uphill battle convincing school boards that their positions are needed as much as the teachers who might be hired in their place. While academic libraries find support in accreditation standards, school libraries have lost some important battles in this regard. In general, public library use tends to rise during a recession because of the plethora of free services they offer communities. That means, however, that the library staff must do more with less. Additionally, library boards are questioning the need for professional positions that are not essentially supervisory.

Most types of libraries are handicapped by the fact that decision makers are not heavy users of their services. In the corporate environment, top management may be unaware that many of the reports produced by administrative assistants and lower-level managers are actually the work of librarians. However, special librarians are becoming much more savvy about documenting and marketing their accomplishments. Numerous studies have confirmed that librarians' research and organizational skills, as well as their knowledge of computer databases and automation systems, have a direct relationship to the profitability of businesses. The ability to review huge amounts of information and analyze, evaluate, and organize it, enables decision makers to focus their efforts more strategically. Librarians in all types of libraries may possess computer skills that, coupled with their other strengths, allow them to be successful in positions with titles like systems analyst, database specialist or trainer, Web developer, and local area network (LAN) coordinator. Nevertheless, librarians may not need to be tied to a library to be successful. In fact, breaking loose from the library environment and creating new titles for themselves may considerably improve their prospects.

Public Perception

In this time of tight budgets, we are especially conscious of how librarians are perceived by decision makers outside the library. We have only been partially successful in overcoming the dowdy, "uncool" popular image of the librarian while the image of a computer or information professional is altogether different. This means that library job titles that were in use twenty or thirty years ago are generally the most vulnerable when it comes to budget cuts. Similarly, positions associated with maintaining specific kinds of collections like periodicals and government documents are in greater danger than those more clearly associated with computers or trendy services for library users. The situation for librarians is somewhat different than for members of other occupations in that their jobs are dependent not only on the library's actual needs, but on funding bodies' perceptions of their needs.

Public perception also plays a role in downsizing some positions to paraprofessional or clerical status. Decision makers may not see the more demanding aspects of librarians' positions or they may not value them. For example, university administrators may view time spent on research and publication as wasted if they do not view librarians as faculty members. In many cases, however, it is librarians who shoot themselves in the foot. Their job descriptions may contain numerous duties that can be done by a staff member with an associate's degree or even a high school diploma. In many instances, computers have eliminated some of the more complex tasks in professional job descriptions, and the more demanding tasks have not been documented. When outsiders view the library staff, they may assume that those staff members with supervisory responsibilities are the only ones worthy of higher-paid positions since this tends to be true of the business world. Library directors are, therefore, faced with the difficult task of defending professional positions and making the case that

- jobs consist primarily of professional responsibilities (in other words, responsibilities not found in the job descriptions of clerks or paraprofessionals);
- jobs include substantial decision-making authority;
- jobs are central to the provision of basic library services used daily by patrons (not simply available should they be needed);
- jobs or the responsibilities they entail cannot be outsourced at significant cost savings;
- automation cannot reduce or simplify these responsibilities to the extent that they could be folded into other professional job descriptions or performed by lower-paid paraprofessionals.

NEW GRADS

If you are a recent LIS graduate or will soon become one, you're very likely feeling a lot of anxiety about the job market. In fact, you may even be wondering if you chose the right profession. How will you compete with experienced library professionals who have built hefty résumés and who have what might be called an inside track? In other words, they are more likely to know what's been happening in libraries and what skills are in demand.

Actually, you would probably be surprised to learn that many experienced librarians who have been flung into today's job market are nearly as unprepared as you. Librarians have often worked in the same library for many years, and they may know little about what's happening in other libraries. Of course, they attend conferences and meet with colleagues. You probably do the same. In fact, if you haven't been attending library conferences, now's the time to get into the habit. Take advantage of opportunities to meet with librarians from diverse libraries. This is where you are most likely to hear about trends in the field. Listen closely for new programs and services but listen even harder to discover the problems they are experiencing.

Becoming a Problem Solver

I emphasize problems because this is where you may find your niche. What do I mean by problems? The last conference I attended, I found myself in a discussion of digitization projects. What began as a workshop ended with much wringing of hands. Libraries are currently under a good deal of pressure to digitize their unique collections. Although "free" money is far from plentiful these days, there is a fair amount of grant and government funding available for this purpose. State libraries have often received funding to spearhead projects, and they in turn prod the public libraries in their state to get to work. Faculty members imagine that academic libraries can put everything on the Web and exert their own brand of pressure. The library may respond enthusiastically by sending a librarian and/or technical staff member to a couple of workshops like the one I was attending. It soon becomes apparent, however, that a digitization project requires considerably more work than anyone first imagines and often more specific technical expertise than staff members possess.

The next time a librarian resigns or retires, the library may decide to restructure the vacant position. If digitization has not lost its appeal, the library director or department head may incorporate it into the job description. There may be duties that can be eliminated or swapped with other staff members. In the end what emerges may combine traditional librarianship with a new high-tech emphasis, and it may be a position that has a new grad's name on it.

Solving Technical Problems

Library administrators and search committees are always looking for new staff members with better computer skills than those possessed by the current staff. Considering that the average academic librarian is in her 50s and the average public librarian is only a little younger, it follows that they have taught themselves to use computers. Our profession began using computers earlier than a lot of occupations so we may be somewhat more computer literate for our age. However, senior librarians did not grow up with modern technology and though they've attended many workshops, they have never had an opportunity to develop any degree of expertise in some specialized or sophisticated area of technology. The younger graduate who has actually taken semester-long courses in database design, website management, or digitization has a significant advantage over librarians who have only dipped their toes in the waters.

I'm going to express a prejudice here that may be somewhat unfair. I have spent time looking at the curricula of a number of MLIS programs, and some of their technology offerings look positively prehistoric. Syllabi and reading lists are often posted online and one actually finds readings with copyright dates in the 1960s. LIS faculty are as old or older than other librarians. It has been just as hard for them to update their knowledge and skills as it has been for their colleagues in the trenches. They can read books but they have few opportunities to learn practical skills. Thus, they have a tendency to emphasize theory—and dated theory at that. On the other hand, I've discovered some outstanding courses that were clearly designed by people who know what's going on in the library world right now.

If you're a new grad applying for a job, it may be assumed that you grew up with a computer chip embedded in your brain. You just naturally know about these matters that are boggling the brains of older librarians. This is a misconception you will do well to encourage. Making yourself into a technology problem solver may be one of the best ways to become a successful job candidate. In truth, you too may need to take some hands-on, cutting-edge courses in specific computer applications. Look carefully at the technology offerings in your LIS program. Do they really prepare you to do something useful in today's library environment? Can they give you the skills to go into a job interview and present yourself as the answer to at least one of the library's technology problems? If your program doesn't offer such courses, you're going to have to improvise.

Other Jobs for New Grads

What about other opportunities for new graduates? Obviously, this is a time when the job market is at low ebb and you may be thinking that beggars can't be choosers. However, your early professional positions will tend to typecast you in the future. To the extent that you are able (in other words, without depriving yourself of food, shelter, or other necessities), apply for positions that stand a good chance of doing well in the future. Remember, you are beginning from scratch and you have a unique opportunity to mold yourself into any type of librarian you choose. Because your résumé is almost a blank page, relatively small experiences take on additional importance. By highlighting certain courses, workshops, conferences, and internships, you can create a fledgling specialist. This is an opportunity that experienced librarians encumbered by long years of experience can't take advantage of.

FREQUENTLY ENCOUNTERED OPENINGS

No matter whether you are a recent grad or a thirty-year veteran, you will need to market your skills in a way that libraries will find attractive. If at all possible, brand yourself as a breed of LIS professional that is gaining, not losing in popularity. So how will you do it? You've probably been haunting job sites, but try to look at the announcements of openings with new eyes. In fact, it would be a good idea to get out pen and paper and make a tally of the number of openings you find for each area of responsibility. The largest group on your list will probably be in management, whether directors, assistant directors, or department heads. Of course, new grads are not yet qualified for most of these jobs, but bear in mind that they are out there. Gradually acquiring supervisory experience is one of the best ways to prepare yourself for the future. If you're a more experienced librarian, one of these jobs may have your name on it. However, you will need to identify enough leadership and supervisory experiences in your background to make your case. It may also be possible to add new credentials like courses in management. They needn't be library management, so any community college or university program would probably fill the bill.

Notice that a number of positions have the title "reference librarian" but if you look closely at the responsibilities involved, there doesn't seem to be much actual reference involved. That may be because job descriptions have often failed to keep up with the rapidly changing library environment. The same job may be called "public services librarian" in another library. It may be a sort of generic entry-level position or it may have very specific responsibilities that require specialized skills. Also notice that responsibilities for a large number of positions, no matter what their titles, include several mentions of computers. These positions may be similar to the ones described above in that when positions became vacant, new computer responsibilities were tucked in before the openings were advertised.

Technology-Related Jobs

If you were to tally all the jobs listed on a popular online job line or in an LIS journal, you would discover that a lot of the jobs fit into the general category of technology-related. Here are a few titles:

- digital services librarian
- digital collection services librarian
- electronic access librarian
- e-access and serials librarian
- ILS (integrated library system) librarian
- knowledge access management librarian
- systems librarian
- e-access and serials librarian

If you're an experienced librarian, you probably understand the problems that libraries are experiencing with technology. If you have some knowledge of the subject, you know where the holes are in library staffing. For example, libraries depend heavily on young technicians who may have good computer skills but may also pose some of the same supervision problems as college work-study students. It takes an excellent supervisor to work effectively with such staff members, translating library needs into terms they can understand and making it clear how important those needs are. Unfortunately, if you have not updated your technology skills, you may imagine that one individual, perhaps with the title of systems librarian, takes care of all the library's technology issues and other library professional jobs remain unchanged. This is a false assumption. Computerization has expanded into every aspect of the library's operation, and probably every newly available professional position includes heavier technical responsibilities than it did even two or three years ago.

Working With Children and Young Adults

What's a poor librarian to do if he can't pass himself off as a computer whiz? One of the jobs I'm betting will survive and prosper is young adult services. Although technological and societal changes have spelled doom to some library specialties, they have boosted others to prominence. Working mothers and the demise of many structured activities that once occupied preteen and junior high students have created a void that the library is ideally suited to fill. If you're planning to go to a library conference in the near future, plan to attend at least one YA program. I think you'll find a level of vitality and creativity that is almost unique among conference attendees. If you honestly enjoy working with this age group, I'm convinced you can expect a long and happy career. Of course, you're going to have to master some fast-paced video games, but you'll have plenty of help from expert players.

Children's services is another area that will not be disappearing anytime soon, but societal changes have had a different impact here. Working mothers are no longer available to bring their younger children to the library, and daycare providers make fewer field trips because of liability issues. Nevertheless, parents are usually the public library's most vocal supporters and they can also be hugely influential in saving the jobs of elementary school librarians. If you enjoy children, have a flair for the arts, and get a kick out of turning a simple story into a theatrical tour de force worthy of Shakespeare, this may be the job for you.

DECLINING SPECIALTIES

Continue noting areas in which libraries are still hiring and then consider what you don't see. In other words, begin with the process of elimination. Take cataloging, for example. You probably won't see a lot of libraries looking for catalogers unless cataloging and systems are linked. Since catalogers were usually the first librarians to use computers, they often became the systems librarian by default. With the passing of time, systems responsibilities increased and cataloging decreased. Records now exist for most books that have been published in most modern languages. Original cataloging is needed mainly for digitization projects, but these are generally small special collections. Such collections will continue to grow, but they do not occupy a central role in most libraries. It's hard to imagine an ongoing need in this area.

Similarly, there are still openings for government documents and periodicals listed, but not many unless the positions have been expanded to include responsibility for electronic services. There are still jobs that need to be done for which professional expertise is required. However, they are either pojects that will soon be completed or that are no longer viewed as central to the library and its future. Of course, we've long been aware that these are not up-and-coming areas of librarianship, but what other areas should a new library professional avoid? Which jobs are not likely to emerge from the recession with the same health and vigor they enjoyed before hard times descended on libraries?

To answer this question, it may be more useful to look at the library through the eyes of someone less sympathetic and supportive than yourself or your colleagues.

The Impact of Computers

No matter what the state of the economy, there will always be people, whether voters, administrators, or local politicians, attempting to tighten the library's budget and identify positions that might be eliminated. It will be helpful to ask yourself how they might view any given position. If they were delving into the innards of cataloging or periodicals or documents positions, they would be looking at jobs that once required masses of paper records; they would be looking at jobs that once required sophisticated research skills to track down missing documents, or determine whether issues of obscure journals were really lost or simply never published. In other words, these penny-pinchers might decide that half or more of the tasks that once called for professional skills have now been simplified or eliminated by computers.

Ask yourself what other professional positions come close to falling into this same category. For example, bibliographers can track down elusive manuscripts, privately printed books, and similarly hard-to-find scholarly works. However, a well-crafted keyword or title search in WorldCat and other databases now retrieves in minutes much of the literature that once took days or weeks to discover. Of course, bibliographers can bring order to a welter of confusing sources by virtue of their subject expertise and knowledge of the complex and chaotic world of publishing. Like catalogers and periodicals librarians, however, the need for their services has been sharply reduced. The history professor or PhD candidate can now achieve reasonably good results unassisted and with minimal effort from his home computer. No one need reinvent the wheel because first-rate bibliographies are shared online. Bibliography is a large part of the job description of many subject specialists, and commercial databases have tended to make subject-specific searching skills less important. Therefore, subject specialists will need to identify new value-added services if they are to prosper in the twenty-first century.

BEGINNING A SECOND CAREER

Some students have come to librarianship from other occupations. Perhaps you've been a physical education teacher or a businessman or a bank teller for the past twenty years. You've been changing over the years, and now becoming an LIS professional seems right for you. That may mean that whatever you used to do seems unappealing. You're excited about your new start and new career and you're not much interested in the past. This may be the way you are feeling at the moment, but it's not the best attitude to take with you into the job market.

If this is your second career, you are bringing with you a wealth of experience that can be repackaged with your new LIS credentials into a winning résumé. It's safe to say that you possess knowledge and experience that a library needs and may not have available.

Your challenge is to identify crossover skills and expertise and then create a marketable package from your assorted qualifications. Somehow it will all go together to make you the perfect candidate for the job. Again, however, you must have the technical qualifications employers expect in a new grad. If at all possible, extract the courses and mine the experiences from your work history that identify you as a problem solver.

You might try to set up some one-on-one meetings with directors or other LIS managers to better understand what those challenges are. If they understand that you're not looking to them for a job, they may be able to help you see where your background might fit into the big library picture. When librarians have worked together in the same library for a number of years, they start to seem very much alike. They have attended the same conferences, participated in the same meetings, and worked together on many projects. They are even sometimes in the same age group since staff were hired when funding was generous and hiring slowed when budgets were tight. You may come out of an entirely different environment and be able to look at issues from a new perspective.

Despite the challenges we are facing, LIS is still a robust and exciting field in which to begin or revitalize a career. It is undeniable that change has impacted the profession even more dramatically than many others, but we have been able to continually transform ourselves. There is no question that the recession is hurting both libraries and other employers of LIS professionals. We clearly have to do some belt-tightening, but jobs continue to be available to those who know where to look. The demise of some specialty areas is probably inevitable, but others are destined to play a vital role in twenty-first century society.

NOTES

1. EBSCO, "Library Collections and Budgeting Trends Survey," May 21, 2010, www2.ebsco.com/en-us/NewsCenter/Pages/ViewArticle.aspx?QSID=360.
2. Bureau of Labor Statistics, U.S. Department of Labor, *Occupational Outlook Handbook, 2010–11 Edition*, "Librarians," www.bls.gov/oco/ocos068.htm.
3. Ibid., "Archivists, Curators, and Museum Technicians," www.bls.gov/oco/ocos065.htm.
4. ALA Office for Research & Statistics, "New ALA report details economic trends in libraries and 2010 outlook," www.ala.org/ala/newspresscenter/news/pressreleases2010/january2010/outlook_ors.cfm

RESOURCES

Fialkoff, F. "Lousy Job Market, Great Career." *Library Journal* 134, no. 17 (October 15, 2009), 8.
Kniffel, L. "Tech Services Consolidation Looms Over Massachusetts' Five Colleges." *American Libraries* 40, no. 12 (December 2009), 26–7.
"It's Pink-Slip Season for California School Librarians." *American Libraries* 40, no. 4 (April 2009), 15.

Maatta, S. "Jobs & Pay Take a Hit "[Placements & Salaries 2009]. *Library Journal* 134, no. 17 (October 15 2009), 21–9.

Matarazzo, J. M., et al., "The Influence of Private and Public Companies on the Special Library Job Market." *Information Outlook* 12, no. 4 (April 2008), 10–12, 14–16.

O'Connor, L., et al., "Demand and Supply of Business Information Professionals: A Study of the Market from 2001–2005." *Journal of Business & Finance Librarianship* 13, no. 3 (2008), 189–200.

2
HOPING FOR THE BEST
RECESSION-PROOFING YOUR PRESENT JOB

If you're feeling some anxiety about your future, you might take comfort in knowing that you are far from alone. Librarians and other LIS professionals all over the country are reading about funding crises in their communities and discovering that those cuts have found their way to their own library's budget. There's no question that we're going through a painful period, but this is not a time to bide your time, wring your hands, or just wait and see. This is a time for action, and there's a great deal you can do to strengthen your hold on your present job while at the same time preparing yourself for a positive transition to a new job if that becomes necessary.

KNOWING WHERE YOU ARE

Perhaps the first and most important thing you can do is evaluate your situation objectively. Rumors are probably flying around the library that may or may not be accurate. Exactly how bad is the library's financial situation? Even for the library director, academic institution, or local government, this is a harder question than it may seem. Budget cuts often appear to come out of the blue. Sometimes it's a matter of knowing a situation is bad, but not how bad. In other cases, decision makers delay sharing bad news until the last possible moment because of the damage it will do to employee morale.

How much budget cutting can the library do without staff layoffs? Once again, this is a difficult question. In general, administrators try to cut staff last, but this is not always possible. If recent funding has been rather generous, there may be a number of budget lines that can be reduced or eliminated before it becomes necessary to hack away at personnel lines. Because libraries differ from one another so much, there are no firm guidelines, but in many situations it's possible to absorb a budget cut of 5 percent. This may not be possible if the library must contend with a 10 percent cut. Try to discover how much revenue your parent organization—whether university, city government, or school district—expects to lose. Bear in mind that the library staff is not seen in the same light as firefighters, police officers, or classroom teachers, and so cuts may be somewhat larger than in other departments.

As Others See You

Once you have a pretty good understanding of what the library will be facing, it's time to consider how your own job will be viewed. To do this, you will need to imagine yourself as a fly on the wall observing those responsible for balancing the budget. Although temporary and part-time positions tend to fall to the ax first, some full-time LIS jobs are also being eliminated. In other libraries, professional positions may be downgraded to paraprofessional status. When the recession ends, budgets will begin to loosen. Library directors will include new positions in their annual budgets, and gradually the library staff—both professional and paraprofessional—will grow. The cycle will be repeated when local economies falter and tax revenue shrinks.

Let's imagine a library director and/or committee of senior librarians charged with responsibility for cutting one professional library position. Where would they begin? In "real life," it is sometimes easiest to take advantage of a retirement or a resignation and simply not rehire anyone to fill the vacancy. Seniority may also play a big role in the decision, and there may be a reshuffling of job titles after the departure of the most recent hire. Also in the real world, a library director may have had difficulty firing a librarian who wasn't working out, whether because of seniority, red tape, or union rules. A mandatory budget cut may provide the opportunity to eliminate the position and more easily remove the offending librarian.

Unnecessary Jobs

Nevertheless, positions are often eliminated because the library can function without them. The committee mentioned above will be looking at job descriptions, comparing them with the actual work performed by the librarian holding the job, and deciding how important those responsibilities actually are. They consider the day-to-day operation of the library as well as its mission and goals. However, when money is tight, decision makers may postpone goals in favor of practical reality. So let us assume that the committee considers each professional position in turn.

Changing Jobs

Does the job description accurately reflect the work that the librarian with this title actually performs? For example, periodicals is an area of the library that has changed radically in the past decade. Most libraries no longer maintain long back runs of journals, most no longer bind large numbers of titles, and most depend heavily on online subscription databases for their needs. So in addition to coordinating current subscriptions, what is it that the librarian is actually doing?

In some libraries, the time freed up by the transition to online resources has been more than filled by new responsibilities. So many tasks have been added or eliminated that it's not the same job anymore. Some libraries have concluded the job can be broadened to include electronic services (e.g., becoming the in-house database guru, evaluating and comparing database interfaces, negotiating with vendors, and integrating commercial services into the library's website). In other libraries, those responsibilities may have been absorbed into new positions. The librarian holding the periodicals position would become less and less needed.

If the committee were considering this latter situation, of course they would conclude that the position is a good candidate for elimination. Often, however, things are not that simple. Most librarians are conscientious workers and when their responsibilities are reduced or eliminated by technology, they look for other things to do. This is generally a good thing because they have the opportunity to experiment with new programs and services. On the other hand, these added projects may not be important to the library as a whole. They may be more a reflection of the interests of the librarian than the needs of the library. I believe that we are going through a period when quite a few library jobs may fall into this category.

Accurate Job Descriptions

Job descriptions may be revised fairly often over the years but not rewritten. There are no firm rules, but a good job description should account for roughly three-fourths of the librarian's time on the job. Other responsibilities tend to come and go, and one-time tasks come up frequently. However, they should probably occupy less than one-fourth of all working hours. In addition, high-priority responsibilities should always be listed in the job description while those responsibilities not mentioned can be assumed to occupy a lower priority. This is important because performance evaluations should be directly tied to job descriptions.

Obviously, it is possible to arrive at a good decision about the importance of keeping or eliminating a job only when decision makers know what that job entails. The committee described above is going to have a hard time evaluating responsibilities that have been added informally and don't appear in the job description.

Defining Professional Roles

A second question that the committee will probably ask is whether the position should remain a professional one. After all, significant savings could be achieved by downgrading it to library assistant or library technician status. Why should the person holding the position possess an MLIS or other professional degree? What tasks require professional knowledge and experience? Technology has transformed many complex responsibilities into routine clerical tasks. Shared or outsourced cataloging is perhaps the most frequently cited example of this trend, but even materials selection—once the very definition of professional responsibility—has to some extent been replaced by vendor profiles. The periodicals department has been impacted by technology as much if not more than most library functions.

Finally, the committee will try to imagine what would happen if this position ceased to exist. How would it work out if a few of the responsibilities were redistributed among other librarians and the rest simply went undone? Would library customers be unhappy? Would they experience poorer service? Would materials become less available or less accessible? Would the library suffer a setback to any of its important plans? Step by step, the committee would determine which position is least needed, which is least important to the library's successful operation. Once the decision is made, they will then go on to consider the individual holding the position. If she is a senior librarian, there will probably be an attempt made to move her into a different job. If there are no positions available or if she is one of the more recent hires, a layoff becomes likely.

IS YOUR JOB SECURE?

Knowing that this is roughly the procedure that will be followed in your library, ask yourself how your position would be viewed. The following "recession-proofing" checklist covers most of the important issues to be considered:

How long have you been employed by the library? As you look around at your colleagues, would you place yourself in the category of longtime veteran or fairly recent arrival? In general, the fewer years you have under your belt, the more essential your position must be to the library.

Over the last few years, what new goals have emerged as being central to your library? How has the library changed? What new services have been added during this period? What plans are moving forward?

Have you been pivotally involved in these changes? Have you been part of the group that guided these recent developments or that recommended these changes? When people talk about exciting new things that are happening in the library, are they talking about you?

Has your position remained largely unchanged for the last few years? If so, this is not a good sign. The library and its environment have been changing rapidly so your position may be moving further from the hub of activity.

Is your title one that might have been in use, whether by you or by your predecessors, more than twenty years ago? This is not necessarily a bad thing. Trendy new titles are not essential, but an older title may be an indicator that your position was more relevant in yesterday's library than in today's.

Have many of your responsibilities been impacted by technology? Has technology eliminated or simplified many functions? Have you taken ownership for new, sophisticated responsibilities associated with technology like website administration? In other words, you might ask whether technology has tended to "dumb down" your position or expand its scope.

What would happen to the library if your job simply disappeared? Could others pick up the slack without too much difficulty? Could many tasks go undone without much hardship to the library? Would your colleagues agree with you on this point? Try to be as honest and objective as possible. We come to view what we do as important, even essential. However, we've discovered again and again that when crunch time comes, libraries can do without many things they once considered necessary.

Has your job description gotten out of date? Do you actually play a more essential role in the library than your job description would suggest? If so, it's definitely time to update your job description. If you're like many other librarians, you may consider job descriptions unimportant—a necessary evil. This is a time, however, when they really matter. Boilerplate verbiage copied and pasted from online templates will do you a disservice. List what you actually do. Make it clear, if you can, that you have a number of important responsibilities that are integral to the success of today's library.

After updating your job description, does your job still look dated and not very important? How can you change your actual duties to appear more relevant? Are there new responsibilities you can take on to "beef up" the job description? Are there duties that can be eliminated to make more time available for these new ones?

Improving Your Chances

Should you attempt to change your job title? Each librarian's situation is different, but you can bet that many of the people you work with know very little about your job. Your title may be causing them to make assumptions about what you do or don't do. I can remember a situation that happened years ago in my own library. A librarian had gradually assumed a leadership position—taking on new tasks, doing them well, and being rewarded by several merit raises. When a new library director was hired, she arrived a time when the library's budget was being slashed. When she looked at this staff member's salary and compared it to his job description, it appeared that he was overpaid and the job might easily be eliminated. In the end, he lost his job because neither he nor the former library director ever got around to changing his title and updating his job description. Consider whether a change in title would more accurately reflect your own actual responsibilities. Conduct some online research to discover job titles that are used in other libraries that have a more contemporary feel (I might even say a more trendy sound). Be sure, however, that the new title actually corresponds to the work you do. You might also want to consider whether there is any possibility of changing jobs within your library. As other librarians retire or resign, their positions become available. Would one of these jobs be more recession-proof than your own? If you were a library administrator comparing that job with yours, which would you consider more essential to the library?

You and Your Boss

It's important during this critical time to have a good relationship with your boss. Whether a department head or the library director, your boss will have a lot to say about whether you lose your job. Do you make it a point to meet with him often? It is almost axiomatic that supervisors intend to meet regularly with the staff who report directly to them. However, over time, other things come up and meetings are repeatedly postponed. Naturally, you are not always disappointed when this happens. Perhaps you weren't ready for the meeting or did not want to admit that an assignment was not done. Since meetings with the boss were not your favorite activity, you found ways of avoiding them and so your relationship has suffered. Since you rarely spend time together, you know less and less about one another. The boss may not know how much you had to do with a successful project. You are not a librarian with whom he shares insider information. He doesn't ask your advice before he makes a decision. The situation I am describing is one fraught with peril. If your boss does not automatically think about you and your role in the library, he is more likely to leave you out of decisions. Ultimately, he may decide that since he knows so little about what you do, your work must be unimportant.

It's also important that your boss really shares your goals and priorities. The relationship between library administrators and librarians varies from library to library. As fellow professionals, they are colleagues, and librarians usually have a good deal of freedom to initiate their own projects and pursue their own goals. If this is the case in your library, it may not have occurred to you that your boss does not really share your priorities.

What is important to you may not be very important to him, but perhaps he has encouraged you to "do your thing." When it comes time to cut budgets, roles may change. Your boss who believed in group process and rarely made unilateral decisions is forced to assume a different role. He must make personnel decisions alone or in consort with his own boss (one simply does not call a group of librarians together and ask them to decide who will be thrown under the bus). That means that someone you may have considered more a colleague than a boss will be making decisions that will affect your future. It's essential to know how he really feels. Once you know, you can help him to better understand your contribution to the library, and you can also be more supportive in helping him realize his own goals.

Employment Policies and Legal Rights

Do you know your rights? Do you know whether your employer has written policies or guidelines for laying off staff? Are they included in the personnel manual or in some other publicly available document? Do you know who represents you and your interests? Are you a union member or covered under a union contract? Are there less formal practices that have always governed the way your employer approaches sensitive personnel issues—and do you understand them? The expression "Knowledge is power" was never more true. When rumors are flying, getting a grip on the extent of the financial crisis, the actions the library may take, and the options available to you is essential. Take your personnel policy manual home and read the sections that concern your rights. Identify senior librarians who have been through similar periods and ask how layoffs were handled. If your HR administrator is someone you feel comfortable talking with, bring your questions to her. What is most important at this point is separating fact from rumor.

CREATING A PLAN

Layoffs may appear to come out of the blue, but the decision-making process that goes into them is predictable. If you can put aside the paranoia that inevitably accompanies periods of financial uncertainty, you can create a game plan to take you through the next few years and help you emerge from the recession with your career moving forward. Having truthfully answered the questions above, you have a much better understanding of your future prospects.

Assuming you decide that the danger is real, what can you do? If you have worked for the same employer for a number of years and are among the more senior LIS professionals, you are obviously in a better position than your junior colleagues. However, you are most certainly not invulnerable. If you haven't been keeping up with technology and other recent developments, you will need to act quickly to be certain that you don't find yourself put out to pasture or moved into a position that is not of your choosing. If you are a recent arrival, you must work even more quickly and energetically. Job security will probably depend on your taking a number of positive steps to become essential and irreplaceable. Simultaneously, you should be exploring other options. Just as it's essential to remain positive, you will also want to be prepared for the worst. No matter what your situation, effective planning is the real key to landing on your feet.

RESOURCES

"How to Recession-Proof Your Job and Your Finances." NPR.org (January 15, 2008).
    www.npr.org/templates/story/story.php?storyId=18115843
"Recession-Proof Your Job: Recession Survival Guide." *Chicago Tribune* (January 5, 2009).
    www.chicagotribune.com/business/chi-mon-recession-keep-job-jan05,0,1506532.story
Weiss, Tara. "How To Recession-Proof Your Job," Forbes.com (February 12, 2008).
    www.forbes.com/2008/02/12/recession-jobs-economy-lead-cx_tw_0212bizbasics.html

3

PREPARING FOR THE WORST
SENSIBLE PRECAUTIONS FOR UNSETTLED TIMES

While you are taking steps to strengthen your role and become more central to your employer's present and future plans, it will also be necessary to prepare for the worst. Despite your best efforts, your position may really be in jeopardy. A variety of circumstances beyond your control may, in the end, result in the elimination of your position. If this happens, you will want to be prepared with a plan for a relatively painless transition to a new job. You will need to give serious consideration to your future. For example, if you are nearing retirement age, you will want to consider whether this is the time to leave the job market. Will your finances allow you to retire? Is this something you really want to do? Other librarians may be considering a career change; again, it's best to examine this possibility thoroughly while you still have a paycheck coming in.

FACING UNEMPLOYMENT

If you plan to remain in the job market, you will need to prepare for a transition period after leaving your present job and before you are comfortably settled in a new environment. This period can be a very difficult one, both emotionally and financially stressful. It will require tenacity, strength of character, and self-control to get through it relatively unscathed and emerge with both your career and your personal life intact.

In this chapter, we will focus on practical issues related to unemployment. If you think your job may be in jeopardy, you will want to spend this time getting your financial situation under control and making the preparations necessary to reenter the job market. As you may have already discovered, this book includes a number of checklists or what you might almost call to-do lists. Thinking about job loss is stressful. In fact, apart from death and divorce, job loss ranks near the top of the list of stressful life experiences. Your emotions tend to take over when you think about your uncertain future so you must find ways to stay focused on the positive things you can do to better your situation. Checklists can provide a structure for confronting your problems. They can help reduce anxiety and force your thoughts into more productive channels.

Unemployment To-Do List

So let's begin with a checklist of steps you can take now that will make it easier for you to job hunt in the future. Many of the items on this list probably should be attended to even if your job seems perfectly secure.

Is your résumé up to date? When did you last revise it? Résumés will be discussed at length in chapter 8, but for now, it is important to make sure you have all the information you need to revise your own. Since a résumé is mainly concerned with your work life, that's often where the information is stored. A copy of your job description, most recent résumé, and other documents describing your accomplishments need to be kept in your home office.

Are you keeping other important documents like commendations, promotions, and awards at work rather than at home? Most of us aren't sure of the answer because our office files consist of a mix of documents. Some of them concern just the library and others describe our work and accomplishments. Because you received that evaluation or award while at work, you may have automatically filed it there. These are documents that need to be taken home. If you need to refer to them at work, make a copy but keep the original in your personal files. Believe me, when you leave that fatal 4 p.m. conference with your supervisor, you will not be in any mood to sit calmly at your desk going through your extensive files. Once again, it may be a good idea to use your home address and personal e-mail account in your contact information.

Staying Connected

Are important files documenting your career advancement, professional development, and other achievements stored only on your work computer? Again, we tend to keep work-related files at work. You've frequently had to prepare for annual evaluations, job reclassifications, promotion, and tenure reviews. You've created documents on your computer that contain essential information about what you've done that justifies job advancement and/or a change in pay grade. This information is also important when you apply for future jobs. Over time, you tend to forget what you have actually accomplished, and written documents are needed to jog memories.

Do you have complete information, including e-mail addresses and phone numbers, for all your professional contacts? Whether you keep your contacts on a Rolodex or in a computer program like Microsoft Outlook, you absolutely must have a copy at home. These contacts comprise your professional network. They are the people you may one day ask for references or information about openings in other libraries. You will want to keep communication channels open, socializing with former colleagues and staying connected to the professional grapevine.

How can you keep your e-mail messages if you are laid off? Your account probably contains hundreds or even thousands of messages including contact information for libraries, library organizations, discussion lists, faculty, committees, workgroups, and colleagues in other libraries. If your job is terminated, you will lose your e-mail account and all that data will be zapped. You have a right to retain messages addressed to you, but how can you do it? Copying your contact information and individual e-mail messages to a personal flash drive is one option. Another solution is to automatically send a copy of all messages to another e-mail account. To do this, you will need to learn how to create message rules in your particular e-mail program. It's a good idea to create a free e-mail account on Google or Yahoo! just for this purpose.

Are your library association memberships up to date? If you become unemployed, your memberships will become even more important to you so you can't afford to drop them. A great deal of information about job openings is disseminated by professional organizations and conferences are among the best opportunities for networking. Your library probably pays the annual dues for some memberships. Make sure they are paid well before memberships expire and you may want to consider paying for additional associations out of your own pocket if they would be useful to your job search.

Are you a member of the more popular online discussion lists in your field? A great deal of informal information about jobs is exchanged on these lists, and official notices of job openings are often posted too. Message posters often include complete contact information in their signatures, information you may someday find invaluable.

Have you considered becoming a member of a social networking site like linkedin.com? LinkedIn hosts dozens of library groups and provides opportunities to get to know many librarians who may be able to provide helpful information. LIS alumni groups are also well represented.

Discovering Job Openings

Do you know where job openings are posted for librarians in your field? Special library positions, for example, may not be posted on library websites. Instead, they may be found with job openings for medical, legal, or corporate personnel. School library openings may be listed on local government websites. Begin casually checking job sites just to get a feeling for what is out there. Bookmark the good ones in your home computer browser. Spend some time reviewing the resources available on the American Library Association's JobLIST site. Check some of the openings in your field and consider whether you have the qualifications needed to compete successfully.

How would you prepare yourself to be a stronger applicant if you were applying for openings like these? Do you possess the technology credentials listed in many job openings? How would your technical qualifications compare with those of other applicants? If you have been in libraries for many years, how do your technical qualifications compare with recent LIS graduates?

Should you be using this time to improve your job qualifications? Could you take some computer courses at your local community college? If you received your LIS degree many years ago, your courses may now seem archaic. Would it be possible to take a few online LIS courses from universities with accredited programs?

FINANCIAL MATTERS

If you lose your job, it's safe to say that you will not be at your sparkling best. When you're under stress, you tend to make bad decisions so you would be wise to make as many of them now as possible. Since financial decisions are among the most stressful, create a money management plan while you are feeling relatively sane and sensible. While you're job hunting, it will be necessary to pay your bills, keep a roof over your head, and keep the wolf from the door. Will you be prepared to make the best financial choices and take advantage of whatever benefits you may be entitled to? Do you know how much money you have in what are usually called liquid assets? How much do you have stashed away in savings? How much cash is available in your nonretirement investment accounts? Are there other places where you have money or other assets stored away that could be easily converted to cash?

What other assets do you have? Some are obviously more liquid than others. You should not touch your pension or retirement accounts if at all possible. Penalties are high and you will be shooting yourself in the foot for years to come. You may have other assets, however, that could be cashed in without doing irreparable harm to your future solvency. Do you have possessions that are no longer needed? Collections that are gathering dust? What are they and how could you use them to help pay the bills during a period of unemployment? You needn't do anything immediately except lay the groundwork.

Keeping Yourself Afloat

Get yourself and your family into shape, financially speaking. Pay down your outstanding bills and don't incur new ones. Explore ways to reduce your monthly expenses. For example, you might ask yourself whether you really watch all those premium cable channels. Could you save money by rolling your telephone, Internet, and cable into one bill? Are there some steps you can take to lower your monthly utility costs? Are your home and automobile in need of some preventive maintenance? Are there ways to increase your rainy-day fund, like eating out less often?

Create an austerity budget designed to kick in the day you learn you will be laid off. In other words, you've been tightening your belt gradually in ways that aren't very painful. If your paychecks will soon stop, more desperate action will probably be needed. Take a good, hard look at your expenses. Find a paycheck stub and jot down the amount of the check. This is probably the sum you're spending each pay period. If you lose your job, this is the money you will not have available. Go back over your bills and other expenditures to determine how this money is now being spent. Keep going until your total expenses equal the amount of the paycheck.

If you lost your job tomorrow, which of these expenses must continue (mortgage, utilities, etc.)? Which could be eliminated (clothes, entertainment)? What ongoing services could you cancel? For example, you will need high-speed Internet and good phone service for job hunting, but losing cable, Tivo, or NetFlix will probably not cause any permanent harm. Keep going until you know how much money you must have to remain solvent and reasonably well fed. If you pay bills online, check your bank statements carefully to see if there are some forgotten monthly deductions. Now compare your resources (liquid assets and anticipated unemployment benefits) with your expenses. Can you afford to remain unemployed for as long as a year? If not, an emergency plan is even more vital.

Unemployment Benefits

Find out how much you can expect to receive in unemployment benefits. Instructions for calculating the amount are available at www.ehow.com/how_4464449_calculate-unemployment.html. Estimating the amount precisely is difficult because there are so many variables like the state you live in and whether or not you have children. However, you can arrive at a fairly good estimate. Note that the economic recession has resulted in the creation of a large number of websites designed to help you deal with unemployment. Many of them are excellent, and you should begin bookmarking the better ones. However, there are always people willing to take advantage of a crisis to make money. You're a librarian and you know better than most people how to evaluate a website. Don't allow your anxiety to cloud your good sense. Stick to the free sites and beware of any that try to sell you something. Don't quit. Sometimes, when we're under stress, we do foolish things. Because everyone on the library staff is feeling the same pressure, they may not be at their best. Arguments and hurt feelings may have become common. Nevertheless, do nothing to jeopardize your unemployment benefits. If you leave your job voluntarily, you will probably be ineligible and those benefits could be all that will be standing between you and the poor house.

TAKING CARE OF YOURSELF AND YOUR FAMILY

If you should lose your job, you will lose your health care benefits. What other options will you have? Is now a good time to put the whole family on your spouse's plan? How might recent health care legislation affect you and your family? You will be able to continue your present health care coverage with COBRA, but it may be expensive. The whole subject of health care is complicated so do your research now. It's essential that you and your family maintain good coverage, but you may have some other choices.

While you're taking care of all these practical tasks, don't forget that you're going through a very stressful time and if you really lose your job, it will get worse. Take a good look at your personal life and consider whether there are things you can do to make it more satisfying and enjoyable. Are you spending enough time with your family and friends? Are you really having fun on the weekends? Are you taking time to really talk with your spouse or partner? Your work is only one part of your life, and it should not be allowed to interfere with your personal relationships or your enjoyment of life. Stress can make you feel tired so you may need to push yourself a little harder to keep in touch with friends. Get together for lunch, and plan date nights with your significant other.

Getting In Shape

You and your family are in this together, and remaining close to one another will help all of you get you through this difficult time. As you think about your family, you might consider whether they're prepared for the rough seas that may be ahead. Are you all physically fit? Stress can take a heavy toll on your health so good health habits are more important than ever. Are you getting enough exercise? Might a walk before work improve your outlook? Remember that treadmill that's gathering dust in the basement? Why not bring it up to the family room? If you smoke or drink heavily, this might be a good time to cut back. Nevertheless, you will not want to pile stress on top of stress so moderation may be preferable to abstinence. What about mental health? Apart from the anxiety you're feeling over your job situation, do you generally feel good about yourself? Are you noticing any signs of chronic depression? Are family members getting along with one another? Are there areas of tension that need to be addressed and would family counseling be helpful?

Making Financial Decisions

Does your family have a system for handling money that minimizes conflict? Who pays the bills? How are financial decisions made? If this has been an area of discord, it's important to work out compromises now because problems will only escalate later. Family members are never in complete agreement about how money should be spent. Compromise is essential, and understanding one another's personal needs is key. What seems extravagant to you may be essential to your spouse's sense of well-being. Both of you need some freedom to make your own choices. There should never be one person who makes all the sacrifices while the rest of the family continues as if nothing has happened.

I remember some time ago reading about the Shakers who flourished during the nineteenth century. I was particularly struck by the words of their founder Mother Anne Lee: "Do all your work as though you had a thousand years to live and as you would if you knew you must die tomorrow." Of course, losing a job is a very minor crisis when compared to losing one's life, but there's much to be said for the sentiment. There's no point in crossing your bridges before you come to them, and you may be looking forward to many years with your present employer. However, if a layoff is inevitable, the best thing to do is face it and move on. Change invariably offers opportunities, even opportunities you may not have sought. Whatever happens to your present job, you have a rewarding career ahead of you if you can stay on course.

RESOURCES

Reeves, R. K., et al. "Job Advertisements for Recent Graduates: Advising, Curriculum, and Job-seeking Implications." *Journal of Education for Library and Information Science* 51, no. 2 (Spring 2010), 103–19.

Sanders, L. "Are You Ready for a Pink Slip? No Time to Fret; Be Prepared." *Advertising Age* 78, no. 2 (January 8 2007), 28.

Stafford, D. "Preparing for a Pink Slip." *Women in Business* 61, no. 2 (April/May 2009), 23.

Wolgemuth, L. "Thinking About the Unthinkable." Special issue, *U.S. News & World Report* 146, no. 4 (May 2009), 46.

4

WHEN THE AX FALLS
FIRST AID FOR DEALING WITH SUDDEN JOB LOSS

Even if you have been hearing about pending layoffs for months, you're usually unprepared for the actual moment when you discover that your job will disappear. Most of us prefer to avoid facing unpleasant truths, and when we get together with our colleagues we tend to reinforce one another. No library administrator wants to talk about the subject, so in the absence of authoritative information, we continue to hope for the best. If you've ever been a supervisor, you know how much you hated to be the bringer of bad news. In fact, telling a staff member that she will be let go is probably the most unpleasant job a director or department head will ever have to do. Naturally they put it off. When staff members voice their anxiety, they try to comfort them, minimizing the danger. In fact, their own supervisors may be doing the same thing, so they themselves don't know how bad the situation has become.

YOUR UNEMPLOYMENT FIRST AID KIT

Budget cuts are often made quickly. No one knows how bad things are until they suddenly became an emergency. Some huge number of dollars must be slashed from the budget by Wednesday morning, so administrators will closet themselves in seclusion and burn the midnight oil. Whatever the process, a staff layoff always produces stunned individuals who feel the ground dropping out from under them. Few experiences in life can throw us into a panic quite the way losing your job can. This chapter is intended to be a kind of first-aid kit, a step-by-step plan for responding to the problem in a rational manner and working your way toward a solution. It assumes that you took to heart the advice in the last chapter. Even if you decided they were good ideas for someone else, it is still possible to start pulling your life together. This is no time for licking your wounds. There's work to be done and it must be done immediately. Let's take it from the top, from the moment when you are confronted with grim reality, and keep moving forward until you have a fully developed plan.

Check Your Legal Rights

Do you fully understand your legal rights? Is there any chance that your termination violates your employment or union contract? Have you achieved a kind of permanent status like tenure that gives you more job security than others who don't possess it? Is your library under any obligation to find you another job if your own position is eliminated? If your job is actually being eliminated, there may be little you can do, but make sure you explore your options fully. If you're in any doubt, go over the library's personnel policy manual. Make an appointment to meet with your union rep if you have one. If you think your rights have been violated, you may need to contact an attorney. Not all legal professionals are up to date on employment law, so it is important to make sure the one you choose does this kind of work on a regular basis.

Can You Negotiate?

Can you negotiate for somewhat better terms? Is a severance package available? How long will you continue to be paid? How long will the library continue to pay your health insurance? Is it possible to make these provisions somewhat more generous? Your own boss may have some discretion in these matters, but you will also want to make an appointment with your human resource director. I do not mean the secretary or administrative assistant, but the HR professional who fully understands the situation.

Talk with your HR representatives about state and federal programs for the unemployed, but understand that they may not have current information. Just as you've always known where to find accurate information, use your LIS research skills to discover more options. Find out if you might be eligible for a retraining program that would allow you to take courses and update your skills. Computer courses may be exactly what you need and they are very likely to be covered by such programs. Check the Department of Labor's website at www.dol.gov for more opportunities.

Take It Slow

Avoid a sudden departure. Remain on the job as long as possible. You may feel as if you'd like to leave immediately and never return, but you have a lot to do. Try to arrange to remain on the job for at least two weeks or preferably a month after you are notified that your position has been terminated. This is becoming increasingly difficult to do in some places because local governments and universities are afraid of employee retaliation. They have instituted practices like changing computer passwords just before an employee is given notice, and requiring that terminated employees leave by 6 p.m. on the day they receive their notice. In some situations security officers even escort employees off the premises. If you must leave quickly, you will inevitably leave important matters undone, and your job search will be hindered as a result. Work with your supervisor to come up with a reasonable arrangement. Don't make him feel guilty or uncomfortable, and make it clear that his job will be easier and the library will be in better shape if you can close out your responsibilities in an orderly manner.

Is it possible to work part time for the library as a temp or a consultant? Would such an arrangement increase or decrease your stress? It might bring in some money and force you to maintain a productive routine, but you would be seeing all those people whose jobs were not eliminated. You might feel just a tad resentful and they might feel a tad guilty. Nevertheless, you would have all the library's resources at your fingertips.

How do you feel about a part-time paraprofessional position? Libraries are open long hours, and they often need substitutes and people willing to work nights or weekends. The advantage of such a job is that you are a member of a library staff. Networking is easier if you see other librarians frequently, chat over coffee, and are able to stop by a colleague's desk to ask for a reference. Investigate how this would affect unemployment benefits.

Get Those References

Immediately request written references from colleagues and supervisors. Academic librarians may wish to get faculty references, and special librarians should obtain references from their clients and corporate associates. Pick up the letters as soon as possible. Be sure you've collected them before your last day of work.

We'll discuss the need for references a little later, but bear in mind that you and your situation are in everyone's thoughts. Your colleagues and your superiors are concerned about you and will usually do everything they can to help you. As time goes on, other subjects will occupy their minds. This is a difficult time for them; in fact, their own jobs may be at risk. Now while you have their undivided attention, get whatever you need, whether letters of reference or contact information for useful members of their professional network.

Apply for Unemployment Benefits

Your state may have a waiting period, and it can take a few weeks to process your claim. In some states, you can file over the phone but be ready with all the information you'll need. If you can't apply by phone find your nearest unemployment office (check www.unemploymentoffice.net for a list). You're going to need your Social Security number, alien registration card (if you're not a U.S. citizen), mailing address, and phone number, as well as the names, addresses, and dates of employment for the last two years. Your benefits will be based on your former salary, so be sure you have pay stubs or other evidence of earnings. Remember that you usually don't qualify for unemployment if you quit or are fired. Make sure you and your employer are in agreement about your situation before you file. Bring the termination letter you received from your employer. Get one now if necessary. Requirements vary from state to state, but if a letter isn't part of your documentation, it's possible that your benefit check will be held up while the unemployment office contacts your former employer. Bear in mind that you must be looking for work. Of course, that's precisely what you will be doing, but when you apply for benefits, you should find out what kind of evidence your local office wants to see, and how and when you should contact them.

Sometimes people forget that unemployment benefits are taxable. In some states you can have the tax withheld from your checks. Consider whether you need the money now or if it's more important to plan now for the time when you may have even less money.

Continue Health Care Coverage

If you haven't done so already, transfer yourself and your other family members to your spouse's health insurance plan. If that's not possible, apply for COBRA through your human resources office. You have the right to continue health care coverage at group rates for eighteen months when coverage is lost due to job loss. It may be more expensive than health coverage for active employees if your employer now pays a part of the premium. The new health care legislation is too new to comment on now, but be sure to investigate provisions that may apply to you. The important thing is to make sure health insurance remains in force since it is not uncommon to have health issues when you're under stress. If you should let your coverage drop, you may have difficulty getting coverage later, or it might be extremely costly. Learn more at www.dol.gov/ebsa/faqs/faq-consumer-cobra.html.

If you file a joint tax return, adjust the amount that is withheld from our spouse's check for income tax. Consider what one paycheck plus one unemployment check will mean to your tax status. Your household will be bringing in less money this year, so your tax rate will probably be lower. Decide whether you can wait for a refund or you will need the money sooner. Another way to increase your family's monthly income is to temporarily discontinue your spouse's 401(k) contributions, but think twice before you make such a decision.

Impose a Spending Moratorium

Put all unnecessary purchases on hold. Review the financial plan you made in the last chapter. If you skipped it, go back and do it now. Plan to be laid off for up to a year. Go cold turkey on shopping and spending until you know exactly where you are financially and what you can afford to spend each week. Believe me, your stress level will be lower if you know you can weather the storm. Treating yourself to a luxury to raise your spirits will only make you feel guilty tomorrow. Prioritize your bills and pay housing expenses like mortgage and utilities first. Late fees can mount rapidly, and you certainly don't want to chance losing your home.

Your financial plan should help you manage your existing debt. The best strategy is usually to pay minimum monthly payments on your credit cards and other loans until you are back at work. Recent credit legislation limits the fees and other charges that credit card providers levy. However, if even minimum payments are impossible, don't delay; try to negotiate a new payment plan. It's usually in a bank or other creditor's interest to keep you as a paying customer rather than lose money if you should declare bankruptcy. If you'd like to talk with a credit counselor, contact the National Foundation for

Credit Counseling at 800–388–2227 or check their website at www.nfcc.org. They can probably connect you with a counselor in your area.

Look at other regular expenses. Canceling insurance policies is usually a bad idea since you may have to pay a lot more when you resume coverage later. Contact your company and find out whether they make special accommodations for people who are out of work. For example, some will give you a thirty-day grace period. You may not need it now, but it's important to be prepared.

Spread the Word

Don't keep it a secret. Let people know that you are unemployed. Make it clear you're not looking for pity, but seek helpful leads from anyone who might have useful information. So many people say that they found their job through networking, that you can't afford to miss what may be your best opportunity.

Begin the job hunt immediately. We'll talk about this in much more detail in the next chapter, but don't delay. Without a job to look forward to, you're not going to enjoy a vacation, and inactivity often leads to depression. Plan to spend your usual workday on your job hunt, scheduling your time just as you would when you're at work. Job hunting is a real job and ultimately you will get paid for it. Don't take time out to grieve the loss of your job. Put yourself on a schedule that is as tight as it was when you were going to work every day. You may be in for a lengthy period of time while you look for another job. Make it as positive and productive a time as possible.

A SHORT LIST OF DON'TS

Now that we've covered the things you will need to do immediately, I should mention some things you definitely should not do.

Don't tell off the boss. Now is not the time to settle grudges or have a temper tantrum. Even if you do not list your boss as a reference, many prospective employers will contact her anyway. They will want to know whether you left your last position in good graces or if there is another side to the story. Your boss is feeling sorry for you and perhaps feeling a little guilty. Take advantage of the situation by putting her to work. Make use of her professional network; she may have contacts who can help you. When called by a library director or search committee member, you want your boss to do everything possible to help you get the job. Don't burn any bridges with your colleagues either. You will want them to keep their ears open for you and make sure their dear former colleague is well informed.

Don't gossip about your job or your boss to outsiders. When you must discuss the job in an interview, keep the bitterness out of the conversation. It's a great library with a great director and great staff. This may sound a little too much like Pollyanna, but the new boss or search committee wants to know how you will get along in their library environment. The best indicator that you will work well with your new colleagues is a positive track record.

Don't isolate yourself from your friends, family, and colleagues. In fact, it's a good time to make new friends. You might join a face-to-face or online support group. It's reassuring to connect with other people who are looking for work, but a wide variety of social groups will be helpful as well. You might consider joining the library's book group or a group for writers or the local quilters. Hiking and cycling groups combine social contacts with healthy exercise. This is going to be a difficult time for you, so you may not always be your own best company. Try to get out of the house at least once every day. The more contact you have with other people, the more optimistic and upbeat you're going to feel.

RESOURCES

Fitchard, K. "Coping with Unemployment" [survey by TelecomCareers.net; graphs]. *Telephony* 242, no. 6 (February 11 2002), 24.

Judkis, M. "How to Beat the Job-Search Blues." *U.S. News & World Report*, 147 no. 5 (May 2010) p. 28.

Thomas, T. "Boomers Take Note: Wealth Fades Quickly For Many Retirees" [EBRI study]. *National Underwriter* (Life & Health/Financial Services Edition) 109, no. 8 (February 28 2005), 25.

5
STEP BY STEP
A JOB-HUNTING PRIMER

To be perfectly blunt, this chapter is intended for the shell-shocked. The first day after losing a job, most of us are not functioning very well. We walk around the house in a daze, reliving all the unpleasant experiences that led up to our present unemployed state, like the moment when we received the termination letter or the meeting when our supervisor broke the news. We go over little things again and again, wondering whether this or that would have made a difference.

PREPARING TO JOB HUNT

This chapter is intended to keep you moving and productive at a time when you may not be thinking very clearly. It is a step-by-step guide to initiating an effective job hunt, and I'll try to make it as specific as possible. If all goes well, you'll soon be chugging along on all cylinders, but for now, let's just take it one step at a time.

Step 1: Create a work space

You'll need a desk, a computer, a file cabinet or file box, a telephone, and a bookcase or shelving. You'll find that a landline is almost essential, and your service should include call waiting, call forwarding, caller ID, and voice mail. These are no longer expensive add-ons. In fact, if you shop around, you may find a provider that includes them free of charge. Cell phones are too unreliable when so much is at stake and a dropped call can mean a dropped opportunity. Your desk should be next to your landline so you can see your computer screen while you're on the phone. Be sure you have a comfortable desk chair because you're going to be spending many hours in it. You may need to do some furniture rearranging, and you may even need to dedicate a room to the job hunt. If there's usually lots of hubbub at home, a door that you can close to write, concentrate, and take part in telephone interviews becomes a high priority. It's also important to have one place where you keep all the bits and pieces of information you're going to acquire. When you're under stress you lose things, so it's essential to have one place where all those clipped job announcements and vitally important, handwritten notes.

Step 2: Check your computer equipment

Most job hunting tasks require a computer. Make sure yours is a recent model that's been well maintained with regular antivirus scans and shows no signs of self-destructing in the near future. Remember that computer hard disks become unreliable at about three years. Even though money is tight, you're going to have to give yourself a budget for job hunting. It is a real job, much like the library position you're seeking. It will require at least as much time and organization, and a modest amount of money. Get what you need, but don't go overboard. The basics are fairly inexpensive, and a new computer can be purchased for approximately three hundred dollars. It's not worth taking the chance that all your hard work could go up in smoke or a poof of electrons. In fact, it's nice but not necessary to have both a desktop computer and a laptop. However, they must be synchronized with one another on a daily basis. There's nothing worse than preparing for an interview and discovering all your information is at home on another computer. Make sure your printer can both scan and photocopy. Again, printers are very cheap, so it's not worth doing without these features. Good, reliable Internet access is another must. Now is not the time for a dial-up or super slow connection. If you're aware of any computer problems, get them taken care of now.

Step 3: Order supplies

Once you have your basic equipment, consider what kind of office supplies you used at work. Since you're going to approach job hunting in an organized, professional manner, think about your desk when you were working. You're not going to have that supply cabinet available when you need a manila envelope or file folder, and you don't have time to run to the store every time you need something. When you were working, you periodically chose supplies from a catalog or an online office supply vendor. Do the same right now. Make sure you at least have the basics: stapler, staples, paper clips, tape, Post-it notes, copy paper, stationery, pens, pencils, note pads, etc. Be sure you keep a supply of postal stamps, priority mail envelopes, and other mailing supplies. Buying your own inexpensive postal scale means you won't have to wait in line at the post office.

Step 4: Set up your files

You'll need to develop a system for dealing with both paper and electronic files. Creating a system for electronic files can be challenging, and a lot of the information you'll be gathering will be in different file formats. When electronic information is stored all over your computer in different types of files, it often gets lost. The first rule of job-hunting success is "Don't lose it!" For example, websites are bookmarked, e-mail messages are stored in the e-mail program's own folders, and letters are saved to "My Documents."

Of course, it doesn't work for all your information, but I find it easiest to copy and paste a lot of information into a database. (If you are more familiar with spreadsheets, they can serve the same function.) Use your database for keeping track of which positions you've actually applied for, what you sent out, and whether you've received a reply.

You can paste the entire job announcement into a database field, and even copy e-mail correspondence and log phone calls. Some of your information is better stored in word processor files, and it is helpful to convert e-mail messages and web pages to this format as well. That way you can work out an organized system and store online information in the same folders.

I interviewed a woman who simply created a single word processor document she called her job-hunting diary. She typed in each day's date and pasted every important message or piece of information she found online. She also copied bits of information from her notebook and Post- it notes. It became a huge hodgepodge, but it was all there. She could usually find what she needed using the program's "Find" command. The important thing is to keep everything together. Experiment with what works for you, but you might want to keep every important file in at least two places. Under normal conditions, this may be excessive, but job-hunting horror stories are common. We can do some really silly things when we're under stress.

Because things are inclined to get lost, scan and make photocopies of your letters of reference immediately. Keep the original in a safe place. In fact, I think it's a good idea to scan many of your paper files and save them in the same electronic folders you set up for computer files. This can be especially useful when you are interviewing far from home. If all your files are together and if you've dutifully synchronized your laptop with your desktop, everything is available at your fingertips. Scanning documents is also useful when you are submitting online applications.

Step 5: Establish daily routines

By all means, keep a to-do list. Use whatever system you're accustomed to, whether you maintain it online in a program like Microsoft Outlook or with paper and pencil. The important thing is that each morning, you arrive early at your home office desk and you begin checking tasks off your list. You schedule the amount of time you will spend and you don't allow yourself to get sidetracked, running to the store for a blue pen, playing Solitaire, or washing the dishes. I can almost guarantee that you'll be tempted by any and all diversions because job hunting is stressful. The more you can make your day seem like a typical workday, the easier it will become.

Think about when you do your best work. If you are a morning person, write those letters immediately since they require the most brain power. Take care of routine tasks later. If you're a zombie in the morning, organize your time accordingly. Give yourself a small reward for finishing a difficult task, but rewards should not become opportunities to escape from work.

Step 6: Follow up on letters of reference

I have never been a fan of the phrase "references available upon request" typed at the bottom of a résumé. Now is the time to confront the difficult issue of references, and I do mean difficult. If your present boss or other references aren't allowed to respond to requests (HR policy), you want to know it. Sometimes an understanding boss will be happy to write a letter or respond to a phone call even if the local HR office disapproves. In other cases, she may obey the letter of the law. You need to know. Employers may suspect (sometimes with reason) that former supervisors invoke HR policy only when they don't want to say negative things about an employee. Since your job has been terminated, you will need clear and convincing testimony that this was in no way your fault.

Ideally, you should have collected your written references while you were still going into work every day. It was easier then to gently nag your boss and other colleagues, and your work computer held the other names, e-mail addresses, and contact information you need. Everyone is concerned about you and usually happy to do what they can to help. Occasionally, you will encounter a supervisor or colleague who is very busy and asks if you will write the letter yourself and they will sign it. This is a golden opportunity, so use it wisely. Don't be embarrassed to write a glowing letter, focusing on the experience and other qualifications that are frequently listed in job ads. If you are interested in more than one kind of job, you might write two letters, each appropriate to a different job. After all, your reference need only sign them. Do show a little humility, however, and ask if there's anything they'd like you to change.

By the time you begin sending out applications, you will want to have several written references in hand, and complete contact information for a few more. If you know that someone is not willing or able to go to bat for you, you have a choice of leaving out that contact information or explaining the library's policy. If you don't think one of the letters does you justice, don't use it.

NARROWING YOUR JOB HUNT

Before you actually begin checking job sites and applying for jobs, decide what jobs you're interested in. You will want to be as inclusive as possible, but you don't want to waste your time.

Step 1: Choose your location

Will you search locally, or are you free to find a job far from home? Are you interested in relocating? Are there specific states or regions that would be acceptable? Are there others that are definitely not acceptable? What about international jobs? Would you like to take advantage of this opportunity to be more adventurous, or is this a time when you must put nose to the grindstone?

Step 2: Consider the type of library

What types of libraries have you worked in (public, academic, school, special)? Are you interested in trying something different? Do your qualifications lend themselves to other types of libraries? Next, what specific job titles interest you? In this tough job market, would you really have a chance at these positions? Could you create a résumé that would put you in the running? You don't want to miss out on good possibilities, but you shouldn't waste your time. There's a thin line between the possible and the improbable. Would you consider a paraprofessional job? If you're a degreed librarian, such a choice isn't usually good for your résumé, but it might be necessary to put food on the table.

Step 3: Make a list

You might want to make a list of job titles divided into two columns. The first column might be what you consider your "A" list— those job titles you're very interested in and well qualified for. The other column would then consist of job titles that aren't perfect. Either they aren't as interesting but you possess the required qualifications, or they really are interesting but you lack strong qualifications. A job title is not worth placing on either list, however, unless you have some reason to believe you could survive the first cut (I'm not referring to specific openings, but to general, widely used titles). Each application you submit should be the best you can do. That means a lot of work; you won't have time to waste on openings for which you are unlikely to receive consideration. Every supervisor has seen hundreds or even thousands of applications that include nothing but a lot of boilerplate verbiage borrowed from a job hunting book or a sample cover letter. I'm thinking of one particular LIS grad who sent out 150 applications using her word processor's mail merge function to insert names and addresses. When no one even requested an interview, she was devastated. Once you have your list, keep it handy. It's intended to keep you focused and grounded in reality. When you're desperate, you begin thinking you could apply for some pretty strange positions.

DEVELOPING YOUR NETWORK

You must know a job exists to apply for it. In most cases, you will want to apply for specific jobs that you know to be available. Blind inquiry letters rarely net results. However, some jobs are never advertised, and others are announced in unexpected places. If there's even a hint of a job opening, you want to know about it.

Step 1: Stay in touch

Be sure you stay in touch with your old colleagues and other librarian friends. They're connected to grapevines that can be surprisingly productive. Let people know you're looking for a job. Don't be embarrassed about it because many others are in the same boat. In fact, you might want to join a group of job hunters, either one that meets face to face or one that gathers in cyberspace. Of course, you can exchange tips, but even more important, you can enjoy the companionship of people who understand what you're going through.

Step 2: Expand your network

To get your networking efforts off to a good start, you might want to begin with an article that's part of the ALA toolkit for getting a job in a tough economy. "Network Your Way into a Job" (www.atyourlibrary.org/network-your-way-job) contains several opportunities that many job hunters find useful. LIS alumni networks are excellent sources of information, especially for recent grads. However, more senior librarians would also do well to stay in touch with their fellow alums. The second opportunity listed in the article is job fairs. Again, this tip may be more useful for new grads who haven't had time to develop a large network of professional contacts.

Experienced librarians know when and where to find useful contacts. The author of the article calls these *warm referrals*. In other words, your own friends and former colleagues probably know many people who might be helpful to you. Library decision makers tend to avoid calls from job hunters. However, mentioning that their friend Nancy Jones suggested you call can open doors. Just be careful to ask for advice and perhaps more contacts, not a job. LIS conferences are a great place for networking because many useful contacts are clustered under one roof. Placement centers of course will be the focus of your attention, but you can learn a great deal from simply chatting in the halls.

Step 3: Get connected

It's a good idea to create a new e-mail account just for job hunting. Use that account to subscribe to all the e-mail discussion lists that are relevant to your area of specialization. Don't forget that venerable list LibJobs (http://infoserv.inist.fr/wwsympa.fcgi/info/libjobs), which has been helping librarians find jobs since 1995. Remember that you will lose your old library e-mail account so if you haven't already transferred your subscriptions to your new account, do so immediately. LinkedIn (www.linkedin.com) is another good source for networking, so become a member and sign up for a variety of LIS-related groups.

DISCOVERING JOB OPENINGS

Successful job hunters have discovered that job openings are not always announced where they expect to find them. It takes an eagle eye and a lot of patience to be sure you don't miss a desirable opening.

Step 1: Identify online job sites

Develop a list of websites you check every day. Most job openings will be discovered online, although a few are listed only in printed library journals. For the time being, focus on the announcements listed online since they have the advantage of being more up to date. It's more likely that the position is still open, and thus worth an application. Most sites list the date when the announcement was submitted, and some are efficient enough to remove an announcement as soon as the position is closed. Be sure to copy and paste the entire content of any interesting ads because it can be hard to find them again. If you're checking a number of websites, one begins to look like another and you lose track of where you saw what.

Below you'll find a small group of websites to get you started, but do use your research skills to discover others. Local job sites are sometimes hard to find, and depending on your plans they may be the most useful. However, one never knows. Some libraries blanket the Internet with their announcements so they will have a large pool of applicants to choose from. Others may search locally or depend on HR departments that know little about the sites where librarians look for jobs. Once a job appears, don't procrastinate. Many job sites are what are called aggregators. In other words, they copy information they find on other sites, so the original ad may have been posted weeks ago.

Step 2: Check out ALA's JobLIST

Your first stop should probably be the American Library Association's JobLIST (http://joblist.ala.org/) both because it has a good selection of jobs, and also because it serves as a portal to useful job-hunting information (the last time I checked, I found 264 openings listed). Something I really like about JobLIST is the availability of employer profiles. There's usually a good description of the library and a link to its website. Also included is a list of all the jobs open in each library so you can decide whether you want to apply for more than one. I also like the "Advanced Job Search" function. This option allows you to choose keywords, as well as city, state, job category, salary range, experience, and required degrees. Information on placement centers at upcoming conferences is provided, and you'll find a wealth of job-hunting tips. A lot of the articles are not specifically intended for librarians, but they may be well worth reading. JobLIST deserves more than just a casual check for new listings. Article links may take you to other job-hunting websites, so it's a good idea to do some sightseeing while you're there. The web contains an extraordinary amount of both information and misinformation about job hunting. You can usually assume that the links on JobLIST will take you to the better websites. Treat it as a textbook, and when you have a little time, make yourself a cup of tea and read an article or two.

To take full advantage of all the resources available on JobLIST, sign up for a free registration. This allows you to upload your résumé, communicate with employers, schedule face-to-face meetings at conference placement centers, create search criteria for jobs, and have the results delivered to you by e-mail.

Step 3: Check larger job sites that list job openings in any location

Other good websites that list jobs include:

- Library Journal Job Postings
  www.libraryjournal.com/csp/cms/sites/LJ/Careers/JobZone/index.csp

- LITA Jobsite
  www.lita.org/ala/mgrps/divs/lita/litaresources/litajobsite/litajobsite.cfm
- Alumni sites like Indiana University School of Library and Information Science
  www.slis.indiana.edu/careers/students.html
- University of Western Ontario FIMS Jobs
  www.fims.uwo.ca/employment/index.htm
- Chronicle of Higher Education
  http://chronicle.com/section/Jobs/61/
- Special Libraries Association Career Center
  http://careercenter.sla.org/
- InfoCurrent (Special Libraries)
  www.corestaff.com/Solutions/Pages/Specialized%20Services/Infocurrent.aspx
- JobWeb
  www.jobweb.com. See especially the excellent article "Where to Find Your Job in the Federal Government," www.jobweb.com/student articles.aspx?id=2263.
- Jinfo (International Jobs in Information)
  www.jinfo.com

Step 4: Check state and regional listings

Many state libraries and state library associations maintain lists of library job openings within their state. State job sites have an intimate feel about them. If you choose to post your résumé, it won't get lost in a vast sea of other résumés. I also find that less prestigious jobs are listed as well as the management level ones. Library employers frequently list their jobs on these sites when they expect to hire locally and have no intention of paying travel expenses.

The following are just a few of the regional and statewide listings of library job openings. An easy Google search like "library jobs" (don't forget the quotation marks) will yield many more.

- Connecticut Library Consortium Jobline
  www.ctlibrarians.org/displaycommon.cfm?an=1&subarticlenbr=23
- Southern States Library Job Postings
  www.libraryjobpostings.org/southern.htm
- Massachusetts Board of Library Commissioners
  http://mblc.state.ma.us/jobs/find_jobs/
- North Carolina State Library
  http://statelibrary.ncdcr.gov/jobs/jobs.html

- Alabama Library Association
  http://allanet.org/resources_job_bank.cfm
- Maine Library jobs
  www.maine.gov/msl/libs/jobjar.shtml
- Arkansas Library Association
  www.arlib.org/job-line/
- Illinois Library Association Jobline
  www.ila.org/jobline/jobline-of-illinois/
- Kentucky Department of Libraries and Archives
  www.kdla.ky.gov/libsupport/jobline.htm
- State Library of Louisiana
  www.state.lib.la.us/public-libraries/library-jobs/
- State Library and Archives of Florida
  http://floridalibraryjobs.org

Step 5: Check local openings

Academic institutions, larger libraries, and business organizations often list job openings on their own websites. County and city governments also list jobs on their websites. First make a list of all the library employers in your area that might hire LIS graduates with your qualifications. A good but incomplete list of library websites is available at www.libraryjobpostings.org/indivlib.htm. However, you know your local employers best. If you're having trouble making your list, ask friends for suggestions. Investigate each, bookmarking appropriate pages on their websites. Checking them at least weekly should be a task on your to-do list.

Remember that LIS grads are employed by a wide variety of employers who may not be tuned in to the library grapevine. For example, hospital libraries naturally advertise in hospital journals and on hospital-oriented websites.

Check Print Library Journals

Although many job announcements have moved to the Internet because of the speed with which they can be posted and made widely available, traditional printed journals still list many jobs that cannot be found online. The reasons why an employer chooses to advertise only in print vary, but you'd do well to simply accept the fact that some still do. More popular LIS journals are available at most libraries, but you must sometimes ask for them as they may be shelved in a staff area. Less widely read journals can usually be found in university libraries. If you are an experienced LIS professional, you are familiar with the journals that colleagues in your specialty are most likely to read. If they are not readily available, you may need to invest in a subscription or join a professional organization. However, in most cases, a lower rate is available to unemployed members.

MAKING CONTACT

As a librarian and researcher, you have an advantage that few other job applicants possess. You're an expert at finding information. If you use this skill to the max, you can increase your chance of success severalfold. You'll be able to learn a lot more about potential employers and can then tailor your application to meet their unique needs.

Step 1: Search libraries and their parent organizations online

Copy the names of senior staff members as well as any information you find on them. Identify special services and programs that the library wants the public to know about. Talk to colleagues and discover what they know about the libraries in question. Treat your job hunt as the demanding job it is and be prepared. Resist the temptation to send off five identical applications in the same day just to feel better and have a sense of accomplishment. Each application is an opportunity, each must be unique to a specific job and a specific library, and each should be seen as requiring an in-depth investigation.

Step 2: Create a website

Since one of your challenges will be to convince employers of your superior computer skills, it's a good idea to kill two birds with one stone. A website serves as both an advertisement for your professional qualifications and a concrete demonstration of your technical strengths. Use your website to make yourself look like an authority in your specialty area. Create a blog or write your own articles. When you run out of steam, provide links to information you've discovered elsewhere on the web. I've actually seen very successful websites that are nothing more than attractively formatted links to good articles on other websites. Be sure to include your résumé on your site with a good, professional-looking photo of yourself.

A great thing about a website is that it can be either plain vanilla or very high-tech. You can demonstrate a knowledge of sophisticated web authoring tools or you can use a beginner's level template that you find online. Both choices can produce a site that you can display with pride. Before you begin, it's a good idea to take a class or workshop at your community college to understand the basics. Many Internet service providers host free websites, but they will want to place their ads on your site. If you can afford it, a better choice may be a low-cost, ad-free website. Google and Yahoo both offer services for small businesses that provide a professional image at a very low cost. If you're a beginner, you might be interested in Yahoo's small business service (http://smallbusiness.yahoo.com/). For a monthly fee, you get very-easy-to-use web design tools that include attractive, professionally designed templates. It's almost as if you're just filling in the blanks. The price includes your own domain name, so instead of a web address that ends "yahoo.com," you can create your own. You can also create e-mail addresses with your own domain name. Once you have your website, include the URL everywhere. Learn how to submit it to search engines so it will come up when people search on your specialty area. Swap links with other LIS website owners, and include the URL every time you list your address and phone number.

Step 3: Become known in the LIS community

If you're a pretty good public speaker, consider submitting a program idea for a local library workshop or conference. A conference program gives you an opportunity to make a positive, professional impression on many attendees.

Step 4: Continue to broaden your network

Being unemployed can make you feel isolated and out of touch with other people. Be sure to spend part of every day on the telephone renewing acquaintances and expanding your social network. There may be days when you feel like becoming a mole and hiding from the world, but this is a time when you must be at your gregarious best. Avoid putting people on the spot and be sure not to sound pathetic.

Step 5: Write articles for LIS journals

This can strengthen your résumé, but even more important, it can give you an excuse to call library administrators you don't know personally. Ask them for their opinions on the topic you're writing about (you can do this for your blog as well). If your article is in your specialty area, you will be updating your knowledge and becoming more familiar with current buzzwords. Even if your article is never published, you can talk with employers and colleagues about something that has a positive, professional ring to it. Telling people you're sitting at home feeling miserable is not going to make you very popular.

Many former job seekers will tell you that the most important step of all is getting your own personal demons under control. Losing a job is a huge blow to your sense of self-worth. Every rejection letter (and you will probably receive lots of them) makes you feel worse. However, in most cases, those employers really knew nothing about the real you. They saw only what you chose to include in a résumé and cover letter unless you were selected for an interview. If you possess the required and desired qualifications, what stands between you and an interview are the words you choose for the application package. Those words are not set in stone. You can change them to respond to a wide variety of situations. You can assume that when you receive a rejection, there was something about that package that failed to impress your readers. Use your personal LIS network to get suggestions. Keep experimenting and keep improving, until you can consistently produce applications that net interviews. It is only then that employers can really see you and the strengths you can bring to the job.

Remember, you will get a job! It may take a long while and it will certainly require a lot of work, but your life will move on. There is a job out there with your name on it.

RESOURCES

Cannady, R., et al. "Making the Best of the Worst of Times: Global Turmoil and Landing Your First Library Job." *College & Research Libraries News* 71, no. 4 (April 2010), 205–7, 212.

Deffree, S. "Life after Layoffs: How to Move Forward after a Job Loss." *EDN* 54, no. 6 (March 19, 2009), Supp19–21.

Farkas, M. "Your Virtual Brand." *American Libraries* 41, no. 3 (March 2010), 28.

Flowers, S. "Get a Job!" *Young Adult Library Services* 8, no. 1 (Fall 2009), 4.

Kulisek, D. G. "Market Yourself to Your Future Boss." *Quality Progress* 43, no. 1 (January 2010), 22.

Miller, B. "Job Search Resistance." *Public Management* 91, no. 11 (December 2009), 4.

6

CHANGING DIRECTIONS
WHEN IT'S TIME TO MOVE ON

Up until now, we've emphasized action because losing your job counts as one of life's most stressful experiences. The floodwaters are rising, and it's essential to keep moving forward until you're on higher ground. However, even though you may be having trouble thinking clearly, you're going to have to make that agitated brain of yours settle down and do some work.

WHY ISN'T IT WORKING

For most LIS job seekers, unemployment is a brief though stressful crisis that will soon be over. If you work hard at the job of finding a job, you will soon be drawing a paycheck again. Largely because of the number of retirements, library layoffs have not been quite as numerous as in some occupations, and some library employers really do have jobs available. There are, however, a significant number of job seekers who aren't so fortunate. For them, the job market is not likely to improve, at least not in the immediate future, and they're going to need to make some difficult decisions. Who are these people, and are you one of them?

A not infrequent reason why librarians can't find jobs is that the jobs just aren't there. These jobs may have titles that have been gradually disappearing from libraries during the past decade because they may not be needed in today's library. Another reason jobs may not be there is that your area has been especially hard hit by the economic recession and will take years to rebound. Perhaps the jobs aren't there for *you* because your skills have become outdated and you are competing with applicants who possess sophisticated technical skills and more relevant educational credentials.

Are You Ready for a Change?

It is possible, however, that your heart just isn't in the search. You are not sure you really want another job like the one you just left. You've grown tired of business as usual and want to explore some other options. This may mean that you're ready for a change in direction. Perhaps you dream of a different career, or you wonder whether it's time to retire. You might even be thinking about the possibility of combining work and leisure in a part-time job or a home business. If you believe you may be ready for a change, this is a good time to explore a variety of possibilities. However, this is not the time to jump into anything without assembling your facts and understanding precisely what you're up against.

WHEN YOU LIVE IN THE WRONG PLACE

The first group we'll consider are the job seekers who live in states that have taken an especially hard hit because of the economy. Although libraries everywhere are being faced with budget crises and the need to downsize, some geographical areas have been impacted more than others. News articles almost daily report drastic cuts in state and local government budgets. Library branches have closed, larger libraries have been stripped bare of staff, and overall unemployment figures are at all-time highs. What sometimes makes the situation especially desperate for librarians in these states is that just a few years ago, the same libraries were doing well and expanding their staffs. Thus, a larger number of librarians were attracted to the area, and now a larger number are affected by cuts.

Analyzing Your Area

It would be helpful to ask yourself the following questions about your own local economy:

- Do I live in close proximity to universities offering LIS degrees? If so, it means that every year there are more new graduates looking for jobs in an area that may already have an abundant supply of LIS professionals.
- Where does my state rank in unemployment statistics? Is the unemployment rate higher than average?
- What drives the economy in my area? For example, in Michigan it's the auto industry, while western state economies are often dependent on energy production. Hard-hit local economies are often those that depend on a single industry or large employer. Do I live in an area where an important industry is in financial crisis? Is there reason to believe that the situation is permanent (an employer has gone bankrupt or moved its operation to Mexico) or will require many years to recover?

Leaving Home

If you've lived in the same area for many years, it can be very hard to pack up and move to a new state or a new part of the country. You and your family have some hard decisions to make:

- Do I really love the area where I'm living? Would I miss my hometown or home state a lot if I were to leave? Would my family suffer?
- How difficult would it be for my family to relocate to an area with a better economy? How would a move affect my spouse's career? What about children? (Schools are among the first to be impacted by financial crises, so your children may actually be better off moving.) Is this a bad time to leave my parents and other family members?
- Could I sell my home, or would I lose all the money I've invested in it? In areas where unemployment rates are high, home prices have often dropped precipitously.
- Would a change in location mean a change in lifestyle, and is this a good or bad thing? Do I feel ready for a change, or would I lose my support system at a time when I need it most?

MOVING TO A NEW JOB

If, after asking yourself these questions, you decide that a major move is right for you, the next question is naturally; where will you go? Just as you have enjoyed an advantage over job applicants in other occupations because of your research skills, you can use these same skills to find areas where jobs are more plentiful. Don't forget, however, that quality-of-life issues are just as important as employment. Even though you're feeling desperate, you don't want to sacrifice your happiness and sense of well-being.

Choose a More Stable Economy

Take a look at state unemployment rates and choose several states near the bottom of the list that appeal to you. Find out why these states are doing well and check on living costs. It will take some time for you to recover financially from this period of extended unemployment, so this is an important consideration. A lower cost of living means you can also look at jobs with lower salaries. Lower income will be balanced by lower expenses. The cost of living in different parts of the country can vary so sharply that you might be forced to live in something approaching poverty in one area while you could be very comfortable in another. If you own a home in an area with a high cost of living, even selling at a loss could provide funds to purchase a new home and perhaps a little extra to help pay bills.

Are there a lot of LIS graduates in the area you're considering? This usually occurs when there are nearby universities offering LIS degrees. In general (although there are some exceptions), the farther you live from an accredited program, the less competition you'll encounter. However, the areas that lack LIS programs may also be less populated and have fewer libraries. You'll need to check it out, but it's not a bad idea to make yourself a map that shows the location of all major programs.

Consider the Quality of Life

Next find out how the areas you're considering compare when it comes to quality-of-life issues. A website like Best Places to Live (www.bestplaces.net) or Gallup's Well-Being Index (www.well-beingindex.com) can tell you a lot about schools, transportation, public services, medical care, and recreational opportunities. Local chambers of commerce can be useful as well. Of course, the chamber has a somewhat biased point of view, but the basic information you need for your investigation is readily available. You should find data on climate, industry, employment, medical facilities, schools, and churches. You can discover a lot about a town or region if you read between the lines and let your imagination flesh out the dry statistics. Compare the information you find with your own area.

Next, begin checking job ads in the areas you've identified. Are there significantly more jobs advertised than in your own locale? Does it seem as if a lot of the job openings are concentrated in a few areas?

Find Information Beyond Your Network

In general, it is more difficult to job hunt far from home. You no longer have your social network of local information professionals looking out for you and there's no one you can call to get the inside scoop. You don't know anything about the political environment, and your knowledge of the economy is second or third hand. You're almost entirely dependent on what you can find on the Internet, although that amounts to quite a lot of information. Interviews cost money, and someone must pay for them. Either employers limit their out-of-state interviews because their budgets are tight or they expect you to pick up the tab yourself. You'll want to be pretty sure that you really want a position before you spend hundreds of dollars on plane fare and hotels.

Plan a Visit

Occasionally, a reconnaissance mission is called for. Plan a trip to an area in which you're especially interested and call a number of employers to see if you can arrange informal interviews. Emphasize that you will be in the area and you'd like to get their take on local libraries, the job market, and the area in general. While you're visiting, try to imagine yourself as a resident. Is this the kind of community where you could feel comfortable? It's a good idea to make a short list of your basic requirements for a new community. Focus on non-negotiables and make it brief since you aren't in a position to be too choosy.

DISAPPEARING JOBS

Another reason you may be in for a long spell of unemployment is that your kinds of job have been disappearing steadily from libraries and the recession has only hastened the trend. As discussed earlier, catalogers, government documents librarians, and others whose responsibilities revolve around one type of media (like film librarians) may fall into this category. Your challenge is to rebrand yourself, and this can be difficult if you've held the same position for a number of years.

Is the Market Still There?

This is a time when networking with other librarians is vital and it's especially important that you stay in contact with other job seekers. Are they getting more interviews than you? Are they getting jobs faster, and have you been unemployed for a longer period of time? If you have been working diligently and sending out well-crafted applications, then it may be that there simply aren't as many openings in your specialty. Librarians in your situation have usually been in the profession for a number of years and so you've had time to get to know a lot of colleagues, many of whom have held jobs similar to yours. They may also have somewhat similar qualifications. What has been happening to them? Are they still at the same jobs? Have they acquired some up-to-date skills that make them more marketable? Have their titles changed? Have they deliberately rebranded themselves to get better-paying jobs or to make their jobs more secure?

Rebrand Yourself

If after you've made your informal investigation and have decided that jobs with responsibilities similar to yours are no longer popular, what can you do? Your best course may be to recreate yourself as a qualified applicant in a more marketable area. Since you've been poring over job announcements, you have a better idea of which job titles appear frequently. Which of these interest you? When you look at the required and desired qualifications, which seem to be more like yours? Do most of the qualifications look familiar but you encounter a few unfamiliar terms? That can be an indication that you're out of touch. If it's been fifteen or more years since you completed your LIS coursework, it might be a good idea to go back to school, either to a brick-and-mortar university or to an online academic program. Before you do so, however, take some time to get in touch with your own university's LIS placement office. LIS career counselors know what employers are looking for and which coursework and other qualifications are in demand. They most often work with recent grads, but will usually be more than happy to help more senior alums. You don't want to commit yourself to a lot of extra work unless it's going to pay off, so don't make a snap decision to return to school. Take advantage of the professional advice that's available to you.

Look Beyond the Library

You might want to bear in mind that even after the recession, LIS job growth is expected to be higher outside rather than inside the library. As I mentioned in chapter 1, the *Occupational Outlook Handbook* predicts good prospects for nontraditional careers. Just consider: everyone in every business, government agency, and research facility is dealing with information overload. They need someone to help them cope with all that information, and that's precisely what LIS graduates are trained to do. Take for example the jobs of corporate digital archivist, digital asset librarian, or digital asset manager. These titles may or may not be listed on the job sites you regularly check, but they are jobs for which you may be qualified. All three normally involve managing a company's digital assets. If you were to add a course or two in database management to your existing qualifications, you might have a new and rewarding career ahead of you.

TECHNOLOGY ISSUES

A third reason that job interviews may not be coming your way is the employer's assumption, either accurate or mistaken, that your computer skills are not adequate for the position that is available. This is an especially difficult problem to deal with because when it comes to computers, we don't know what we don't know. A highly trained technician can look down from her lofty heights and be aware of all the skills and knowledge she has acquired. The librarian who has not ascended to those heights can see little. She has learned only the computer skills needed to perform relatively low-tech tasks and may have no idea that more sophisticated skills even exist.

Discover What You Don't Know

How is it possible to determine whether you are not getting jobs because of your limited computer skills? You might first think about the role you played in your former library. Were you the one who helped other staff members with their computer questions, or were you the one who had the problems? Did you frequently call library technicians and other staff members when something peculiar happened, or did you troubleshoot your own computer? Have you mastered a sophisticated database program and are you the one who answers rather than asks the questions about it? Have you created a website? Have you helped to make the technical decisions about the organizational structure of your university's digital library? Have you been involved in an imaging project? Have you selected networking equipment? On every staff, there are LIS professionals who are called in to share their expertise when computer decisions are made and others who have difficulty even understanding the resulting decisions. If you are in this latter group, it is now time to remedy these deficiencies.

RADICAL CHANGE

Of course, there are a variety of other reasons why some people are unable to get jobs, but perhaps the real reason is that you are just not sure this is what you want to do. Perhaps you've held similar jobs for many years; you've lived in the same place, and you've become somewhat bored and dissatisfied. Is it time to retire, start a new career, or choose a plan of action that represents a less drastic change, but will still revitalize your spirits?

Are You Ready for Retirement?

Let's begin by considering whether retirement is a viable option. Since you've already spent quite a bit of time analyzing your finances, ask yourself whether you can really afford to retire. If from this point on you were to live on your pension, investment accounts, and Social Security benefits, could you maintain a comfortable standard of living into your 90s? (I once found a chart that showed life expectancies for occupations that included librarians, and as I recall, we can expect quite long lives.) Take into consideration that some of your income sources will be fixed and unchanging. Other sources may rise and fall depending on economic conditions. Remember that you have some flexibility now. There are a variety of ways in which you can earn some extra income, but this may not be the case later on.

Combine Work and Leisure

For this reason, you may want to negotiate a compromise between full-time employment and retirement. For example, you could reduce your workload and earnings, leaving at least some of your retirement income untouched. As a general rule, you can assume that the longer you wait to draw on your various income sources, the more money you will have later. Your retirement accounts will continue to earn interest and your annuities will yield higher returns. If you were born in 1943 or later, you can increase your Social Security income by 8 percent for each year that you delay retirement up to the age of 70. If you choose to collect Social Security benefits before you reach full retirement age, you can expect a hefty penalty. Plan for a long and active life. If you are like many people, you did not get serious about a savings program until fairly recently, so you may not have accumulated thirty or thirty-five years' worth of assets. Don't allow the desperation you may be feeling now to influence your decision, but do remember that you probably have many options you haven't considered.

Know What You're Getting Into

Next consider other ways in which you may or may not be a good candidate for retirement. Are you already involved in hobbies, outdoor activities, and other interests that occupy a large part of your time, or do you rarely have time to do anything but go to work and later collapse in front of the television? Successful retirees are usually busy retirees who now have the time to do more of what they always enjoyed doing. If you look on retirement as an opportunity to travel and lounge on the beach, think again. Travel is expensive, so you're not likely to be able to travel more than a few times a year. Lounging quickly becomes boring and does not provide a basis for a satisfying lifestyle. If you don't have a more concrete, well-developed plan for retirement, you may be more focused on escaping from something that makes you unhappy rather than embracing a new lifestyle.

Understand Your Options

If this describes your present outlook, why not consider some other options? The following list begins with active retirement and moves on to a variety of possibilities that combine work and play, and future earning power.

Retire with a clear plan to achieve some long-held goal. Perhaps you have been involved with a nonprofit group in your community and retirement would give you the opportunity to devote more of your time to this project. Perhaps you are a writer who has been working on a book project. Retirement would free up more time to write.

Phase in retirement gradually. For example, you might look for a job in a location where you hope to retire. This will give you an opportunity to get to know the community before you make a permanent commitment. You might choose a job that is not really on a career ladder but which might allow you to gradually reduce the number of hours you work each week.

Find a part-time library job. In the present economy, this can be a problematic choice because part-time staff are usually more vulnerable to layoffs than full-time staff. Nevertheless, libraries that don't have sufficient funding for a full-time position may be able to squeeze out enough money to hire a part-timer.

Become an independent contractor. This is a choice that might work well for special librarians. They might be hired for particular projects, for example the digitization of some corporate records. They might produce a newsletter describing the latest trends and intelligence in a field. Academic librarians are often English majors and might consider freelancing for their university and other employers, editing or proofreading university publications. There may not be a lot of money in freelancing, but there's a lot of freedom, and freedom may be what you need at this phase of your work life.

Go back to the classroom to learn new skills. Having known many LIS professionals over many years, I've discovered a common characteristic. We seem to like going to school more than other professions. Of course, this doesn't apply to all of us, but a surprising number find the prospect of continuing our education extremely appealing. Several of my favorite role models did this with great success. One became an architect in her 60s, and another earned a PhD when he was just a few years younger. For both, it was a struggle but also a joy. They complained that it was hard work forcing their brains to learn new things, but those aging brains came through for them in a big way, and the sense of accomplishment they experienced more than made up for the hard work.

Launch a new career. Even if you don't go back to school, you can choose to pursue a new career. Most librarians have spent many years interpreting computers and other technology to help their users. They serve as both teachers and go-betweens, translating the language of computer technicians into words that their library customers can understand. They know how to find information on almost anything, and information is the most valuable currency in many environments. If you've always been attracted by a career path, why not spend a little time learning whether it's really what you think it is? (We all have a tendency to see the grass as greener outside our own profession.) Use your research skills to investigate other careers. Where might you fit in? Which of your skills are most relevant?

Start a home or other small business. Technology has given rise to an explosion in the number of home and other very small businesses begun on a shoestring. This is a wonderful choice if you have always wanted to be your own boss, if you have some basic business skills, and if you have a lot of imagination. However, it takes time and money to get a small business started. Not as much money as was once needed, since you can manage a very productive business from your home office or basement with the Internet and cheap but sophisticated telephone services. However, it takes time to develop a customer base, so if you need money immediately, this may not be the best choice for you. If the idea is really appealing, you might want to reconsider it later when you're once again gainfully employed. You might then begin on a small scale, operating your home business as a hobby, devoting some of your leisure time to it, and investing only as much money as you can afford to lose.

Add to this list other options that you've been considering. Why not list the positives and the negatives of each of the options that are actually worth considering. If you're approaching retirement age, you know yourself better than when you were younger and so you're in a better position to make a choice that's right for you. While you're unemployed, you have some time to think about your life and what you want to get out of it. You may not have an opportunity like this (thank heavens, you say) for a long time. Use it productively.

RESOURCES

Anderson, M. A. "Working Retired: Part 1: Refocused and Recharged." *MultiMedia & Internet @ Schools* 15, no. 3 (May/June 2008), 33–5.

———. "Working Retired: Part 2: Building a Bridge to Retirement." *MultiMedia & Internet @ Schools* 15, no. 4 (July/August 2008), 35–7.

Gleason, D. "Where Will You Work? A Five-Year Statistical Analysis of AALL Job Placement Listings." *Law Library Journal* 100, no. 3 (Summer 2008), 529–39.

Rathbun-Grubb, S., et al. "Public Librarianship as a Career: Challenges and Prospects." Special issue, *Library Trends* 58, no. 2 (Fall 2009), 263–75.

Rimland, E., et al. "Transitioning to Corporate Librarianship." *Journal of Business & Finance Librarianship* 13, no. 3 (2008) 321–34.

7
FIRST IMPRESSIONS
APPLICATIONS THAT MAKE THE CUT

At some point in the near future, you hope to be sitting opposite a library administrator or search committee convincing them that you are the best applicant for the job. However, that meeting will undoubtedly be preceded by many, many small steps. The secret is preparation—and that preparation must begin long before the interview.

FOCUSING ON THE JOB AND THE EMPLOYER

Actually, it all begins as soon as you discover the job announcement. Once you've decided that this is an opening you may want to pursue, immediately begin learning more. You'll need to investigate not only the job itself but also the library and the people, especially senior staff, who work in that library. All of us, I suppose, tend to focus on ourselves. The people to whom you are sending your application are thinking not about you, but about themselves and their library. They have a problem—in other words, there is work that's not getting done and plans that are not being implemented. They are interested in how someone might solve their problem and how well that someone might fit into their world. Your task is not so much to tell them about yourself as to focus on their need.

What the Ad Really Says

Begin by examining the job ad carefully. Check to see if there are other versions online (the library's own website may have a much longer and more complete announcement since some job lists charge by the word). You can do this by taking an exact phrase from the announcement, enclosing it in quotes, and pasting it into a search engine. Assemble all the versions you can find and keep your fingers crossed that they were written by a librarian and not a human resource professional. What do they really seem to be looking for? How is this announcement different from others you've seen for similar jobs? In one sense, your challenge is to become a mind reader.

The job that's open in this particular library is unique. In many ways, it's unlike other jobs with identical job titles in other libraries because this library has evolved differently. It has different goals, different needs, and a different cast of characters. Can you read between the lines to discover what these people are really looking for? Focus on them, not yourself. Don't begin comparing your skills and experience with their requirements until you really understand what they are looking for.

Obtaining More Information

How can you find out more about this position? What do you already know about the library? Your friends and colleagues usually provide the best insights, so ask around. Use your social network to get all the information you can. Is this a new position or is the opening the result of a recent resignation? It's helpful to know whether you will be following in someone else's footsteps or helping to create a new position. Have two positions been merged and would you be expected to do both? These situations have their advantages and disadvantages, so it's a good idea to know what you're getting into.

When the Library is Far From Home

At the moment, the job market is far from sunny, so you may be applying to libraries a far distance from home. If this is the case, you're going to have to do some real detective work, and as a librarian you're better equipped for the task than job applicants in other fields. Use the Internet to find out all you can about the libraries in which you're interested—the staff size, the names and titles of senior librarians, budget, etc. Sometimes you can even find the minutes of staff and librarians' meetings online.

If the announcement asks you to reply to someone other than a human resources administrator, find out who that person is. You can probably gather enough information to make some educated guesses about the people who will make the hiring decision. Learning about the human side of libraries will help you better understand what they're looking for. LIS professionals are so well represented online that you can often learn a lot about them as individuals, including their perspectives and preferences. Some of the information will be useful for writing your cover letter and if you make the cut, it will be invaluable in the interview.

Investigate the Community

Also gather enough information to decide whether this is a place where you'd like to live. Find out about the cost of living, especially the cost of housing, the unemployment rate, the schools if you have children, and other quality-of-life indicators. As we all know, statistics can be boring and seemingly meaningless. Don't just look up numbers. What do the numbers really say? Compare them with your home community. Consider whether unemployment numbers are improving or if budget cuts have been so draconian that basic services like education and police protection are inadequate. Be sure to bookmark local newspapers to get a feeling for how residents view their area. Though you may be feeling somewhat desperate, you don't want to have to go through this again. Job hunting takes a lot out of you both financially and psychologically. You're looking for a stable, supportive environment where you can recharge your batteries and grow professionally. There really and truly are jobs that you should avoid.

THE IMAGE OF THE PERFECT APPLICANT

Once you have some basic information about the library and the people who will be involved in the hiring decision, it's time to sculpt the first impression you will make on these potential colleagues. In my experience, we tend to hire people who match our mental image of the perfect applicant. Though it may sound simplistic, that perfect applicant is often the person we see in the mirror. When the library director brings together the group who will conduct the search, they will talk about the qualifications they are looking for. Though positions may have very different job descriptions, the group's wish list can probably be boiled down to the following: a youthful, enthusiastic, energetic librarian with outstanding computer skills who will bring fresh ideas and reinvigorate the somewhat stodgy library staff, while at the same time, not rock the boat.

Youthful Portrait

If you've been a librarian for a number of years, I'll bet you would happily take a penny for each time you've heard similar catchphrases. You might also despair because you don't fit this youthful profile. Fear not, because as I said, we all tend to look for other people like ourselves. We imagine how we ourselves would do the job and subconsciously look for clues that reassure us. And, of course, we don't really consider ourselves to be too old for our jobs. In fact, if someone looks just a bit younger than the way we picture ourselves, we are usually willing to give them the benefit of the doubt. I am absolutely convinced that 45-, 50-, or even 60-year-old applicants can walk into an interview and be that perfect applicant. As long as they appear fit, energetic, and enthusiastic, have taken relevant computer courses, can talk the talk, and have taken care with their appearance and banished the stereotypical image of the aging librarian, they can be that perfect applicant in the eyes of library decision makers.

Neither Too Old Nor Too Young

New library school grads, on the other hand, have a somewhat different challenge. They must be all those good things—young, enthusiastic, energetic, etc. However, they must realize that senior librarians do have this self-image in the back of their minds and they may view 25-year-old applicants much as they view their children's friends. If this is the case, you can't appear to be too young. "Youthful but mature" must become your mantra. (I feel as if I'm telling the story of Goldilocks and the three bears. Perfect applicants don't appear to be too old or too young. They're just right.)

THE PERFECT APPLICATION

It's hard to know how many applications the library will receive for any particular position, but it's safe to say that there will be more than you imagine. Many are from people who are just blanketing the library community with boilerplate cover letters and résumés. They merely waste everyone's time, and search committees don't have time to waste. They can't look carefully at each application, so they look for obvious clues that an applicant is the right sort of person. They also imagine the right person would write a letter much like the one they themselves would write, submit the materials they would submit, and follow the rules they would follow. If you don't follow them, they reason, there must be something wrong.

Different but Not Too Different

That all-important first impression is based on the application package. Successful application packages are somewhat similar to one another and follow established practices. While job applicants in other occupations may use shock tactics to get attention, this usually doesn't work well with librarians. Perfect applicants are a lot like the other qualified applicants for the job, only better. This, of course, makes it difficult to stand out from the crowd.

Nearly everyone in the job market has spent some time looking at career guidance suggestions (at least they should have done so). Thousands of sample résumés and cover letters are available online. Tips for successful interviews are equally available. A whole industry is devoted to producing books and magazine articles to aid job seekers. Together, these recommendations constitute a kind of procedure manual that has become widely accepted among employers. In other words, they have created certain expectations that allow employers to ignore some applications because they don't follow the rules.

Memorable Application Packages

So what are these rules that successful applicants follow? Perhaps the first and most important is "Never dash off a cover letter and résumé on the spur of the moment." The corollary to this rule might be: "Be conscious of the image you present at every stage of the process." Apart from such basics, many of the rules are stated outright or at least hinted at in the job ad. For example, you wouldn't call for information if the advertisement states, "No phone calls." Other clues are more subtle, but noticing and responding to them is an important part of a successful job hunt.

Begin your carefully orchestrated plan with the application package, the written materials you use to begin making your case. You have only these few sheets of paper or lines of text to sculpt an image in the minds of decision makers. Although parts of the package can be used again when applying for other jobs, each application should be just a little different, specifically focused on the job that you're interested in. Of course, the next time you see this same job title in an ad, you will have most of the materials you need at your fingertips. However, that will be a different library with somewhat different needs and expectations. Look for clues in the job announcement and adjust your approach accordingly. If the next job opening you find has significantly different duties and required qualifications, you will need to make substantial changes. There are definitely shortcuts that will save you time when you are applying for a number of jobs, but there are no shortcuts when it comes to research. If you don't understand what an employer is really looking for, your application is likely to find its way to the slush pile.

COVER LETTERS THAT GET NOTICED

Let's start with the basics. Every application should include a cover letter and an employment résumé. Some employers also require that you complete an application form as well. Because the résumé can play such an important role in determining your apparent fit for a position, we'll be devoting a lot of our time and attention to it. Some applicants toss a résumé into an envelope and mail it off to an employer with no attempt to make a unique impression. In other words, the résumé, is forced to stand on its own, naked and stripped of all the narrative information that would help an employer see you as an individual, as someone who might fit comfortably into the library staff. If you were standing before a library director or search committee, you would not shove a résumé in their faces and leave. Similarly, you should never send off a résumé unless it has the support of a well-written cover letter.

Taking Advantage of Your Unique Skills

Making overly generalized assumptions about librarians is always a mistake, but we do tend to be somewhat better writers than members of other professions. We are good spellers and decent grammarians, and we tend to be comfortable in the world of words. This is a huge advantage when it comes time to write a cover letter. To be effective, a cover letter should present you as a unique individual. It should say all the things a résumé can't say about your fitness for this particular position and why you're interested in this particular library. It is your opportunity to sell yourself, and it may be the last chance you will have.

Of course, it goes both ways. The people reading your cover letter will also be competent writers and careful readers. They will be more likely to notice careless grammar and indications that your letter was produced by a mail merge program. However, since they are more likely to be readers than most other decision makers, time spent making your letter interesting and informative is more likely to pay off. Remember that they will be trying to fit you into a pattern they understand. Since they likely have no special expertise in psychology and no crystal ball, they will be trying to learn whether the picture of you they see in your application materials resembles other people they've known who have been successful in similar jobs.

Cover Letter Contents

Most cover letters should fill a single page, but there's nothing wrong with continuing onto a second page. It's my personal opinion that librarians are somewhat more willing to read a longer letter than other employers, but don't stretch their patience. I myself went through a phase of writing three-page cover letters. Although I don't recall that it actually cost me any jobs, it was certainly not a kind thing to do to the poor souls who had to wade through stacks of applications. Nevertheless, your cover letter needs to be long enough to make it clear you possess both the required and desired credentials. Then you will need to complete the picture so that you become as a distinct individual with unique talents and experience. The following is a list of the basic information that every good cover letter should include:

Include the title of the job you're applying for. If you are responding to a specific ad or announcement, the exact title should be included. If not, make it clear that you're not just fishing for any job that happens to be available.

State your qualifications. In the first or second paragraph, make it crystal clear that your qualifications meet *and* exceed the ones listed in the announcement. In fact, it is best to use the actual words in the announcement and bear in mind that the first cut may be made by a human resources administrator who is not familiar with library vocabulary. If you have somewhat different credentials, you might briefly make the case that they are equivalent to the ones in the announcement. However, with the job market as tight as it is, your case will need to be a good one.

Emphasize your updated skills. Make it clear you've stayed current in your field and have up-to-date skills and knowledge to offer the library. Since the letter must be relatively brief, you won't be able to go into any detail, but the quick mention of a successful project, an advanced computer course, or an impressive conference will do wonders.

Point out additional qualifications that may not lend themselves to the résumé format. Showcase one especially impressive or relevant accomplishment.

Expand on information in the résumé but don't repeat. Take advantage of the freedom the letter format provides. A résumé is by definition condensed and somewhat cryptic.

Personalize each application. Mention something you know about the library and its program. Respond to the specific qualifications listed in a job announcement. Again, you might copy some of the language in the ad or job description.

In addition to specific information or what you might call "hard facts," you will want to give some indication of what makes you an interesting person. This is harder to get across in one brief letter.

Entice employers to keep reading. Make sure your letter is actually interesting. While résumés are cut and dried, cover letters should be readable. What would interest other librarians about you? Make your letter attention-grabbing without resorting to extreme measures, and raise your readers' interest level so they will want to further consider your application package.

Express your personality. Communicate humor, success, and optimism. Describe a person who is so interesting that readers will want to know you better. However, avoid mentioning your personal life unless it is relevant to your application and you are certain it will not set off alarm bells with your readers. Don't, for example, mention your age or children. However, if you plan to visit the city where the library is located, say so. It could improve your chances since budgets are especially tight now and the opportunity to avoid paying interview expenses might be attractive to some employers.

Become the "Great Communicator." Communication skills are always an important requirement, so communicate! Make your letter a sample of your superior ability to express yourself effectively.

What Not to Emphasize

One of the most important pieces of information communicated in a cover letter is the reason you are interested in the job. You may or may not have to mention the fact that you've been laid off, depending on the length of time you've been out of work. However, don't leave the impression that you are a failure. Don't spend time explaining and making excuses. Keep the tone of the letter positive and enthusiastic. Why do you find this job exciting? Why do you think it's a perfect fit for your interests and abilities? It's just common sense that the letter is not the time to mention your limitations or requirements. You're creating an image; every word counts. Don't waste time on nonessentials. You might even make a list of your real reasons for wanting the job and then cross off the ones that hint at dissatisfaction or desperation.

If you're an older applicant, be careful that you don't describe a long string of jobs that go back to the dark ages. Because you have had a long career, you have a lot you could write about, but don't. Throughout the application and interview process, use your experience judiciously. Bring up experiences that show how you can solve problems and become be an asset to the new library, but remember that this letter should not make you appear to be older than other applicants. It should simply make it clear that you are the best choice for this particular job. Bear in mind that your readers have a stack of applications in front of them. Your cover letter and your résumé are your two opportunities to sell yourself before your application lands on the rejection pile. This first cut is made quickly, so some very positive bits must stand out. Although I have no scientific basis for my conclusion, I have the impression that librarians begin with the cover letter while human resources professionals first skim over the résumé.

FINE-TUNING THE COVER LETTER

It probably goes without saying that you should get the name of the person to whom the letter is addressed, the address, and the job title perfect in your letter. Be sure there are no errors. Some people couldn't care less how you spell their names; others take umbrage at even a minor misspelling. An error in the job title alerts the reader that this could be a form letter sent to many libraries. Remember that you are the best applicant for this particular job. If you don't even know what the job is or who you're writing to, why should the employer believe that you are the best choice?

Surviving the Screening Process

Because job announcements attract many applicants, an administrative assistant or someone else who is not really involved in the hiring process may be asked to screen the applications. Remember that the screener may not be particularly interested in the opening and is probably in a hurry. That means that he may read only the first paragraph of the cover letter and the top sections of the résumé. He also checks to make sure that each application package contains all the pieces specified in the announcement and may check that applicants possess the basic requirements for the job. If something is missing the screener may have the authority to place the application in the slush pile. If you suspect that your application may be screened before it reaches anyone in a decision-making role, then you will want to construct your cover letter accordingly. Organize it like a newspaper article, with the most essential information at the top and less vital sections lower on the page. Screeners are not as big a hurdle in libraries as they are in the corporate world, but they are fairly common in larger libraries.

Parts to Personalize

Some library applicants customize the first paragraph of their cover letter for each application, but they leave the rest of the letter unchanged, reasoning that the reader will probably read only the first paragraph and will skim over the rest. If they make the first paragraph so strong that it does much of the work of the entire letter, the strategy may work. Nevertheless, the "canned" section of the letter may contain wasted words that are just taking up space. Remember, the specifics of your job history belong in your résumé. This is not the function of the cover letter.

The Professional Looking Package

If you haven't applied for a job in a number of years, remember that computers have raised the bar on application package expectations. Not only must everything be produced on a computer, but it must look slick. Decision makers may tell you that they don't care about snazzy stationery or designer formats, but they are going through dozens of packages. Naturally the ones that look good will catch their attention, and they will gradually begin looking down their noses at the ones that look thrown together.

In recent years, personal computers, career books, and college placement counselors have brought uniformity to the application process, making one application package look superficially very much like all the others. When one stands out, it is usually not for positive reasons. Employers looking for quick ways to eliminate undesirable applicants may eliminate applications that are carelessly written, smudged, or printed in a peculiar type font from consideration. Career counselors even debate the color of the paper. People who are not very familiar with computers are often impressed with the many type fonts that are available at the click of a mouse. A job application is not the place to experiment with artistic-looking fonts, and most job hunters stick to the tried and true Times, Times New Roman, Helvetica, Ariel, or another widely used font. Just as the type of font chosen should not call unwanted attention to itself, neither should the stationery. Choose good quality paper in white, cream, or pale gray.

GETTING HELP

If you are one of those job hunters who usually skips or copies a sample cover letter, you will need some help. Do you have a friend or family member who writes well? If you are uncertain about your own grammar, it is always best to have someone else check it over for you. Spelling and grammar checkers are wonderful, but there are many errors they don't catch. Your amateur editor just needs to be good at details and able to get your corrected letter back to you quickly. If this is a problem that really concerns you, you may find it worthwhile to hire a professional copy editor. Many writing websites maintain long lists of copy editors who work mainly with struggling writers and PhD students. Since these copy editors are likely to be struggling themselves, they are often happy to copyedit your letters for a flat per-page fee. Since a cover letter is usually a single page, the cost is very reasonable. You may simply include the text in an e-mail message or attach a draft of your letter. The copy editor loads the attachment on his computer, makes additions and corrections, then sends the letter back to you attached to another e-mail message.

INCLUDING A PORTFOLIO

Career counselors sometimes advise including a portfolio with your application package. This may or may not work in your favor, depending on your former job and the one for which you are applying. To be effective, a portfolio must be instantly eye-catching. A library director or search committee is not going to read through a report or bibliography and may be annoyed at your adding yet more paper to their overflowing stack. If, however, you have been involved in the creation a website, professional-looking marketing materials, or other attention-grabbing printed materials, then it may well be worth including a small selection with your application.

You can readily see that each application is going to require a lot of work. Job hunting is unavoidably labor intensive, but you can be certain that the work will eventually pay off. Few job hunters land a job after sending out mass mailings consisting of generic cover letters and résumés. Fortunately, these are tasks that you can probably do very well since they make use of both your superior research and communications skills. No one would suggest that unemployment is fun, but try to find satisfaction in learning more about yourself and doing what you do well.

RESOURCES

Bloom, L. M. "Five Tips To Stand Out." *Library Journal* 133, no. 15 (September 15 2008), 35.

Fisher, H. "Strong Cover Letter, Résumé Keys to Getting Noticed." *The Quill* (Chicago) 94, no. 3 (April 2006), 45.

Glasbrenner, G. J. "Preparing for Your Next Career Move." *AALL Spectrum* 14, no. 3 (December 2009) p. 1–2.

Thompson, K. "Cover Your Bases with a Savvy Cover Letter." *Phi Kappa Phi Forum* 89, no. 3 (Fall 2009), 25.

8
COMPOSING THE WELL-TEMPERED RÉSUMÉ

Once you feel comfortable with your cover letter, it's time to turn your attention to that other essential of the application package, the CV or résumé. In fact, the first thing you might want to decide is which term to use for the masterpiece you will soon produce. Most librarians submit résumés, but academic librarians may prefer the term *curriculum vitae* or CV for short. (By the way, those of us who survived high school Latin may assume *vitae* is plural and change the word to *vita*. It is likely no one will know the difference, but it really and truly should be written as *vitae* because of that peculiar genitive case we never quite understood.) If you're applying to an academic library, *curriculum vitae* may be the safest term to use, especially if the announcement emphasizes academic credentials. Library CVs don't differ greatly from résumés, but they place somewhat more emphasis on degrees, research, publications, awards, and languages. Base your decision on what you know about the library.

RETHINKING YOUR RÉSUMÉ

If you're like many people, you have an employment résumé stuffed in the back of a file cabinet or saved somewhere in the depths of your computer. Whenever you apply for a job, you retrieve and update it. Updating has really meant "adding." Each time you were promoted, joined another organization, or received an award, the information was added to your résumé. (At least, I hope it was added. Such information often becomes lost if we don't happen to be job hunting at the time.) Eventually, your résumé has gotten longer and longer. It's probably time to do some serious restructuring and rewriting if it's to become the finely wrought instrument that will sing your praises.

Your Résumé Tells a Story

Although you may view your résumé as just a chronological list of your accomplishments, employers expect a résumé to tell them a story. The story develops from the way they knit together your experiences, mentally filling in holes and answering questions based on their own past experience. In other words, the employer looks for a story of gradual progress toward generally recognized objectives. In the corporate world, this usually means more money, more status, and more power or decision-making authority.

Other career patterns are acceptable within LIS, but they must be evident from the résumé. Most employers understand that both family needs and quality-of-life issues play a role in the choices you make, but they still expect to see clear objectives and steady progress.

The Invisible Job Ladder

Years ago, a friend who held the title of director decided she needed a change. When a new and more interesting position was created within her own library system, one that did not carry the director's title, she applied for it and was hired. It turned out to be a good decision, but years later she needed to relocate for personal reasons. She told me that job hunt was the most difficult of her entire career. Each time she applied for a job, the interviewer spotted this irregularity. Deep down employers believed she had been asked to step down from her director position, thus raising undesirable red flags. Although there was a perfectly reasonable explanation and her boss was more than willing to offer her support when called for a reference, she was rejected for more jobs than she cares to remember.

My friend's situation was a difficult one in that there were not a lot of ways she could get around the change in title. However, an annotated résumé might have clarified her career goals. In other situations, job titles are not so clearly defined, and subtle changes in wording might be perfectly acceptable. At any rate, employers are looking for a pattern of gradual job growth. There are a variety of ways to be both truthful and to structure your résumé to create the desired impression. The secret is making judicious choices about what you include and what you leave out.

Résumé Secrets

Before going any further, I think it's time to divulge a secret that recent grads may not know. If you're a more experienced librarian, you're already aware that almost no one really reads résumés from top to bottom. Libraries tend to be pretty democratic work environments—or at least they try to be. A number of staff members will probably be asked to evaluate résumés. Academic libraries nearly always appoint search committees, and supervisors in other types of libraries usually seek input from other librarians. That means that quite a few people will be sitting at desks stacked with applications, but few of them will be vitally interested in them. The résumé format is not very attention-grabbing and usually somewhat difficult to read. If you have a dozen of them in front of you and if you're not the one who's really responsible for the final decision, you're not going to read very carefully. In fact, for that first cut, you may do little more than skim the upper half of first pages. If they look promising, you might read more. That means your résumé must be constructed accordingly. It must not draw negative attention by looking too different from others on the stack. Yet, it must stand out and draw positive attention to a few choice nuggets positioned precisely where the casual reader would look first.

Listing Experience

How much experience do you want to include? In general, you will want to include all your professional positions unless they lasted for less than a year. Other jobs may be included if you're a recent grad who hasn't had time to build a work history. Career counselors are somewhat undecided about whether to be up-front about your age since there is ample evidence that older job applicants are indeed the victims of discrimination. I'm personally convinced that your age should be left nebulous until you have the opportunity for a face-to-face meeting.

No matter what your chronological age, it usually becomes almost moot when you have the opportunity to sell yourself and your qualifications in an interview. That means your résumé should not call attention to either your extreme youth or your gray hair. A 40-year-old has somewhat less than twenty years experience, and 40 is a rather nice, neutral age. Could your résumé be that of a 40-year-old applicant? Typically librarians remain in the same job for three to five years, so a 40-year-old applicant might list four or five positions in the work experience section. It might be a good idea for your résumé to list roughly this number as well. Include the most recent jobs as long as they produce the impression of gradual progress toward the one you are applying for. If you're a new grad, of course, you may need to do a little honest padding with non-LIS jobs, internships, and even volunteer experience. Obviously, they don't carry the same weight as professional positions, but they tend to make your résumé look like the others under consideration.

Listing Dates

Some employment counselors advise that older applicants leave out dates entirely, but I think LIS employers look for dates as an indication of stability. They wonder whether you have job-hopped or been unemployed in between jobs. If your dates make it clear you have remained gainfully employed, it's probably a good idea to leave them in. It may be necessary, however, to omit the dates of your academic degrees or your cover will be blown. Likewise, if the earliest job you choose to list carries an impressive title, you will probably not fool anyone. Remember that the employer is looking for a pattern of gradual progress, and anyone leaping into a position with a title like chief librarian at the age of 25 defies belief. This strategy will work only if the title and responsibilities listed for earlier positions can, without prevarication, be made to sound relatively unimpressive.

CREATING A RÉSUMÉ FORMAT THAT WORKS FOR YOU

Librarians' job titles sometimes present problems on a résumé. If you've never officially been given any title but Librarian I, some creativity may be called for. In other situations, our jobs may change over the years but our titles don't. In such cases, you might create unofficial titles that more accurately describe your responsibilities during different periods of time. Inventing a title may be acceptable if it actually corresponds to your responsibilities and doesn't make your position sound more grand than it actually is. Even better, develop an annotated résumé that lists your responsibilities in each position. Your library probably has several résumé books in its collection. They provide examples of alternative styles specifically designed to emphasize your more sterling qualities and minimize problems. Take a good look at the way work experiences can be described without making the résumé excessively long.

The Longtime Employees

For the man or woman who has held the same job for the past twenty years, the résumé can also present problems. Either you will appear qualified for only one type of job, or more relevant work experiences from the distant past will call attention to your age. An annotated résumé will allow you to list promotions and new assignments like separate jobs. This strategy not only provides the pattern the employer is looking for, but also gives you the opportunity to describe different skills and responsibilities with each reassignment or promotion. If you really think back, you'll probably discover at least some of the responsibilities listed in the job announcements you have been studying.

Listing Accomplishments

For both older and younger job applicants, creating a section titled "Selected Accomplishments" or some similar phrase near the top of the first page can be an excellent way to get started. First of all, such a section tends to be more readable and interesting than the rest of the résumé. If done well, it awakens interest and encourages your readers to learn more about you. It also tends to mask problems like the ones described above. Take a good look at the résumé that's been gathering dust in your file cabinet. Would it be helpful to make your own list of especially relevant experiences, mixing titles, projects, and responsibilities to create a clearer picture of your qualifications?

Pick the experiences that are most relevant to the jobs you have in mind, listing choice nuggets that are clearly transferable to the new position. Bear in mind that the prime real estate in a résumé is this space at the top of the first page. Employers may not read much more before making their first cut. Therefore, place your most positive qualifications near the top. You might want to create different résumés for different positions, changing only this top section to draw attention to your strongest qualifications.

Ubiquitous Action Verbs

Career counselors often suggest that each item or bullet point in such a list begin with an action verb. This is a good way to inject life into your résumé and get away from a boring list of library names, addresses, and dates. However, having read many, many résumés over the years, I'm convinced action verbs can be overdone. I remember one search committee that couldn't stop laughing at a résumé that sounded like it came from the CEO of Microsoft. The applicant had described her achievements in words she obviously found listed in a job hunting book. However, she was applying for an academic library position, and that vocabulary came from the corporate world where people are more accustomed to marketing themselves aggressively. If she were applying for a job in a corporate library, her résumé might not have occasioned a single chuckle, but academe has a different, more subdued culture.

There's a good list of these action verbs at the Quintessential Career Website (www.quintcareers.com/action_alpha.html), but make your choices carefully. Don't make it appear that you masterminded a large project when you were a team member on a lesser one. Younger job applicants, in your quest to make your experience look more impressive, be sure that you don't inadvertently misrepresent your experience. You'll look foolish if you have to "confess" during an interview.

HOW EMPLOYERS VIEW YOU

In some ways, the whole point of the cover letter and résumé is to get you to the interview stage. Once you have made that initial cut and can actually talk with an interviewer, you will have an opportunity to explain irregularities about your situation. You will have a much better opportunity to present yourself in a positive light. For now, you don't want your résumé to defeat you before you have had an opportunity to launch your attack. The current economic crisis has kept some people out of work for a long time. In normal times, employers look on periods of unemployment with suspicion. Why don't you have a job? What is so undesirable about you that you can't get a job? Employers now understand that many competent library professionals have lost their jobs because of the recession, but they may still have doubts.

Minimizing the Impact of Unemployment

Nevertheless, you cannot deliberately make it appear that you are still working for your former employer. That could be viewed as misrepresentation, and it's certainly not the way to get an interview off to a good start. How can you minimize the impact of unemployment without misrepresenting your situation? When you're listing recent job experience, you may wish to include the year but not the month. This can obscure a period of unemployment (up to a year and a half) until you're ready to talk about it.

I should mention here that if you are blurring dates or listing work experiences like the ones suggested below, you are not trying to fool anyone. You may even mention the layoff in your letter so it is clear you were not fired. However, there's something very off-putting about listing yourself as unemployed on your résumé. The term invites pity and carries with it a sense of inactivity. You want it to be clear that you are far from inactive and are using the time productively to become an even more desirable applicant.

In addition, it may be the case that over the years, you have developed lucrative hobbies or have earned money for doing work outside your regular full-time job. If you own a small business you can, of course, list it as a job. Successful home businesses have become so common that most employers no longer see them as suspect as they once did. Voice mail, fax machines, and desktop publishing programs can convey the impression of a fully professional business enterprise. If you choose this strategy, it's better not to use the term *self-employed*. Instead, list the name of your business and yourself as owner.

Independent Contracting

Another commonly used strategy is listing your job title as consultant during the period in question, but of course, this requires that you actually do some consulting work. Senior librarians are often asked to return to their former library after a layoff to share knowledge or help out in a crisis (yet another reason to leave an employer on good terms). You may choose either to call this part-time employment or consulting. Too often, unemployed executives have listed themselves as consultants merely because they were available for consulting if someone happened to hire them. This has tended to give consulting a bad name among some employers. You might, therefore, wish to list yourself as a consultant to a specific library. Occasionally, library applicants cover a period of unemployment with the vague term *writer*. Once again, this can be somewhat suspect, so clarify what it is you write. Many libraries have outdated (or nonexistent) policy and procedure manuals. You might offer your freelance services to update one so you can legitimately become both a writer and a consultant.

Volunteer Jobs and Internships

Librarians have a somewhat unusual opportunity in that practically every library has a crew of volunteers. A volunteer who is actually a qualified librarian can be a godsend to a struggling library, and the volunteer job can help you shore up your résumé. This is an especially good strategy if you are a recent graduate, want to change your area of specialization, or want to work in a different type of library. A title other than volunteer is preferable if the library is amenable, and many libraries are willing to create a title if you have a specific project in mind and are serious about the work.

Use the experience as a training opportunity and learn the language or jargon so that your description of your duties will make you sound like an insider. Another option is to talk an employer into an unpaid intern position in the library of your choice. Again, most employers are delighted to have free help, and most will work with you on a title and duties. I do suggest, however, that you volunteer in a new library, not the one you're leaving. It's hard not to feel resentful if your colleagues are still on the payroll and you're not.

Become a Student

Consider the option of taking online LIS courses while you are unemployed. Courses at a nearby university are another option. You can list yourself as a student and make it clear that you're using your time to update your skills. Even computer courses at a local community college could be useful if well chosen. You will always be a more attractive applicant if you've continued to update your skills. Worded carefully, your résumé can make it clear that even though you are unemployed, you are actively working toward your goals. If you are invited for an interview, you will have more to talk about than your last job. Keeping an interview upbeat is essential, and you will want to discuss the interesting things you're doing now, not focus on your problems.

RETURNING TO THE JOB MARKET

Women greatly outnumber men in libraries, and women have some unique problems when it comes to applying for jobs. Their résumés often include gaps when they were raising their children or caring for elderly parents (increasingly, men also have such gaps). If they have moved frequently to further their husbands' careers, they may have a number of unimpressive "pickup" jobs, or they may have quit a job because of a babysitting crisis. For example, they might resign in May when their children's summer vacation begins or when the last payment has been made to the orthodontist. If you see yourself in this description, take a look at your résumé as an employer might. Remember that the employer wants to see a pattern of stability and what appear to be reasonable job choices.

Stable Work History

There are a number of ways you can strengthen your résumé while not misrepresenting your accomplishments. For example, short-term employment that produces the impression of job hopping may be working against you. You might, therefore, remove jobs that lasted less than a year unless they are especially relevant to the position for which you are now applying. Removing employment dates is another strategy, but as I mentioned, it's not a decision to be made lightly.

Be careful not to list too many jobs that seem to go nowhere. Consider whether removing earlier jobs might make you look better. The "Selected Accomplishments" section described above can work especially well in this situation. Analyze both your paid and volunteer positions to identify the specific skills that are applicable to the new job. Experiment with wording each as a transferable skill. You can select different skills for different job openings.

Topical Résumés

Even in the work experience section, jobs need not be listed chronologically. Instead, you might create categories, putting similar experiences together under a single heading. This allows you to place your most relevant and responsible jobs at the top of the list. For example, you might call one of the categories "Supervisory Positions." Once you have placed your most impressive positions in the most visible positions, you can further draw attention to them by describing them and listing responsibilities when appropriate. Again, remember that the first page of your résumé is the most important. If you can catch the employer's attention, you may have earned yourself an interview.

Older Applicants

Earlier I mentioned that library decision makers are frequently looking for youthful new hires who will add pep, vitality, and new skills to the library staff. I don't know about pep and vitality (my senior colleagues already seem pretty peppy to me), but there is certainly a need for up-to-date skills. The problem is that libraries have been completely transformed by technology. Job descriptions of today's librarians would sound like a foreign language to LIS grads of the 1970s and early 1980s. In fact, there were no such creatures as LIS grads back then because information was viewed quite differently. Those of us who received the bulk of our education in the days of card catalogs and six-part forms have courses on our transcripts that may be completely useless in today's library. Though our more general courses have helped to shape our library philosophy and professional ethics, more specific how-to courses have become almost totally irrelevant.

FOCUSING ON YOUR STRENGTHS

Whether you are younger or older, never send out a résumé that doesn't enhance your chances of success. Remember that there is always a way to reshape your résumé, to paint the most attractive possible picture of you and your strengths. Recent graduates have the advantage of being able to list courses that are clearly useful in today's libraries, but they lack experience. Older librarians have plenty of experience but will probably need to make their academic credentials look relevant. That means a different kind of résumé for each situation. Employers are always looking for librarians who can take the lead with computer applications and services. You will want to mine every recent course, work experience, workshop, training program, seminar, and continuing education experience in your past and choose the ones that make you appear most technically savvy. Don't list technical qualifications that go back more than ten years since yesterday's computers are now ancient history.

Other Résumé Sections

Every résumé contains a variety of information besides work experience and education. It's really up to you to decide what to include. You're putting your best foot forward, so naturally you'll include sections that work to your advantage and omit others that don't contribute to the image you're creating. Here are some of the commonly used headings:

Career Objective	Continuing Education
Professional Skills	Career Highlights
Conferences Attended	Memberships
Presentations	Affiliations and Professional Associations
Publications	Awards
Special Skills	Extracurricular Activities
Language Skills	Honors and Distinctions
Computer Skills	Current Research Interests
Highlights of Qualifications	Hobbies and Interests
Personal Profile	References
Volunteer Experience	

THE CUSTOM TAILORED RÉSUMÉ

As you can see, the résumé format offers plenty of flexibility. Why not take each one of these headings in turn and list items you could include? Which ones make you look most like the perfect applicant? Which best describe your strengths? Just keep it short. Most résumés should not exceed two pages. However, I have a few personal prejudices about what should and shouldn't be included. I always have the feeling applicants are padding when they list hobbies and interests. However, if they clearly contribute to your "perfect applicant" image, go for it. "Professional Skills" can be a useful category if you've come to libraries from another occupation. The skills you list may look relevant even if the job titles don't. "Personal Profile" is another heading that allows you to position your most positive information at the top of the first page.

Career counselors sometimes caution about looking overqualified. This is not usually a problem in libraries since librarians, especially those in academe, possess a surprising variety of degrees and accolades. Naturally, however, a PhD applying for a library assistant position will raise eyebrows. Consider the type of library to which you're applying and think about whether your list of credentials makes you look too different from other applicants.

Formatting the Résumé

Once you have decided on the content of your résumé, the next question that arises is "How should it look?" Many successful businesses have been built on supplying "knock-'em-dead" résumés to job hunters. The problem is that once you have paid the rather large bill, you have to use up your supply of beautiful résumés. Since they will all be identical to one another, you will be unable to add and change the information to respond to different opportunities. Since I am including some of my personal prejudices in this book, I will admit that professional résumés say "new grad" to me, and depending upon the job that's available, this may not be the impression you want to make.

You would probably do better to type your own résumé into your own word processing program on your own home computer. Choose a simple format from the samples in a résumé book and make sure that you can quickly make changes without throwing all the text out of alignment. Even more important, proofread your résumé each and every time you send out an application package. When you make frequent changes, errors creep in, and additions that were relevant to the last application may simply take up space in later versions. If a required or desired qualification is listed in a job announcement, your résumé should make it clear you possess it, but that may be the last time you have reason to mention it.

Stationery, Type Fonts, and Photocopies

Because it is tedious to carefully check your résumé each time you print it, some job hunters compromise by photocopying a few extras each time they alter their résumé. If you use a good-quality photocopy machine that is not running out of toner or prone to streaks and scratches, this can be acceptable. However, standard photocopy paper is not appropriate for a résumé. Most "copy shacks" will allow you to use your own paper, or you can purchase better-quality paper for this purpose. Business stationery conveys a professional image, so it is a good idea to order your stationery from an office supply company that carries an attractive line. Business executives tell me that both the too-casual photocopy and the résumé printed on paper often used for wedding invitations are equally taboo. Since you're presenting yourself as a professional, your written materials must be consistent with that image. White, cream, and pale gray stationery are all acceptable.

Because you are presenting a professional image, beware of the more imaginative type fonts. Plain old Times New Roman is a frequent choice (black type, not the more artistic brown or navy blue) although many prefer the simplicity of a modern, sans-serif type like Arial or Helvetica. The other 487 fonts that came with your word processor are better used for that homemade birthday card. It's a good idea to coordinate your cover letter and résumé, using the same stationery and type font.

COMMON RÉSUMÉ PROBLEMS

Once you've got your résumé together, check and see if you've managed to avoid common pitfalls and include your strongest selling points.

- Have you keep it short, no more than two pages?
- Have you avoided long lists of jobs that might contribute to a feeling of instability or make you look older than necessary?

- Have you found a way to make your work experiences tell a story of gradual growth and achievement?
- Have you found a way to use the prime real estate at the top of the first page to your best advantage?
- Have you emphasized your accomplishments without looking like a braggart? Inevitably, the format of a résumé encourages or even demands bragging. However, reading about ordinary jobs worded to sound like extraordinary achievements can become annoying.
- Did you focus on the skills and experience that will be most useful in the new position?
- Did you choose optional résumé sections that best showcase your talents?
- Did you proofread your résumé and all your materials carefully each time you sent off an application?

Creating a résumé occasionally makes you aware of weaknesses or holes in your qualifications that you hadn't noticed. This may be a good time to enhance your qualifications with a workshop, college course, professional membership, or volunteer job.

APPLICATION FORMS

Some employers require that applicants submit a standard application form. State governments, for example, may require that you complete the same application as a highway worker or an accounts receivable clerk. Although it is sometimes possible to substitute a résumé for the form, some HR offices insist on them. From a legal perspective, such forms make sense since they usually require the applicant to sign a statement attesting to the accuracy of the information. By signing in the box provided on the application, you acknowledge the employer's right to terminate your employment if you have provided any false information. Another reason that personnel administrators like to use a special form is that it makes it difficult for applicants to evade difficult questions.

Follow Instructions Exactly

If the announcement of the job opening mentions such a form, make sure that you obtain a copy. Don't assume that you can ignore it unless you have been informed by someone in authority that a résumé is an acceptable substitute. Since the form will be just as visible as the other parts of the application package, don't take it lightly. You have no idea of the order in which your materials will be reviewed, so it is possible that the application serves as the basis for the first cut.

Tips for Completing Forms

Making the completed form look neat and professional is your first challenge. Since we don't have typewriters anymore, many applicants will simply sit down with a ballpoint and fill it out on the spot. Just as quickly, it may be consigned to the slush pile before anyone sees your carefully written résumé or cover letter. Spend some time and consider carefully how you will answer each question. Your library may still keep a typewriter for public use. Even better, you might scan the form, save it to your home computer, and insert borderless textboxes after each question. Many employers make their application form available on their websites. Depending on the file format, you may be able to download the form and answer the questions using your own word processing program. However you complete the form, it must look almost as good as your other materials because it has just as much chance of being noticed.

ONLINE APPLICATIONS

Speaking of online applications, we should spend some time discussing this recent phenomenon and consider how to make the most of the opportunity. Many employers are using the Web to streamline the hiring process, while others still advertise openings and look at applications in the old-fashioned way. The savvy applicant must be able to respond to either situation without diminishing his chances for success.

Imagine that you discover a job that interests you on a website. You click on a link and are asked to complete an online form that contains a lot of short-answer, multiple-choice and yes/no questions. You're then asked to attach your résumé and click on a button—and presto, you're finished. This is certainly an appealing way to complete an application with a minimum of effort, but it may not be the best way to present yourself. You might first want to find out whether the employer actually prefers one method of receiving applications over the other. Obviously, you will want to choose the submission method that will receive the most attention. Then think about whether you can present yourself well in an online application. Do the cut-and-dried questions prevent you from emphasizing your strongest qualifications or force you to reveal information you'd rather avoid?

It's easy to click the wrong button or make other mistakes when you are filling out an online application. If the instructions are confusing, you may feel uncomfortable and unable to think of good answers. It's a good idea to compose your responses offline so you can take the time to consider the best answers, then type them out ahead of time. You can paste the text into the online application screen.

The Art of Reaching a Real Human Being

Libraries haven't gotten into recruiting software as heavily as the business sector, but you should nevertheless know that you may encounter it. Large employers like universities and state governments may have purchased applicant screening software that allows computers to eliminate obviously unacceptable applicants to save the time of human decision makers. It is possible, however, that the program may eliminate applicants when a human screener might have been more positively impressed. The computer program may be looking for a specific pattern: a yes response to one question, a no or the absence of certain words in another section. Consider that an online application may have less chance of reaching the desks of library decision makers. Also consider that recruiting software programs sometimes chew up carefully formatted résumés. Convert yours to a PDF file format before uploading it, or simplify the formatting in a word processed document.

Libraries sometimes prefer that you submit an online application because a search committee will be reviewing submissions. Instead of printing out hundreds of pages, your online application can simply be forwarded to everyone involved in the selection process. If all of your materials including transcripts and references are converted to the PDF format, you can be assured that everyone sees the materials exactly as you submitted them no matter whether they use Macs or PCs.

E-MAIL AND FAX APPLICATIONS

Both e-mails and faxes have the advantage of arriving instantly. If there is an application deadline and your package may not arrive on time, both of these methods offer a way to assure that your application will be considered. If, however, you are not struggling to get your application in under the wire, should you send it electronically? First, of course, you will need to know that such submissions are acceptable. Then consider whether the format will change the impression created by your application package. In general, I'm reluctant to fax an application because fax machines are so unreliable. You never know what will be printed or how it will look. A photocopy of a fax is even less attractive.

If you send an e-mail message with PDF files of all your materials attached, all your readers will receive the same information in more or less the same format. Of course readers will not have the opportunity to admire your business stationery, but most application packages are photocopied anyway. If you plan to send an e-mail submission, take as much care with it as you would a printed application. Bear in mind that the e-mail message may end up separated from the attachments. If you treat the message itself as a cover letter, be sure to include it as a well-formatted PDF in the attachments.

Just before you send off an application package, make one last check to be sure everything is included. Check the job ad and be sure you have the items that are both required and desired. Even though you're sending complete contact information for all your references, it's wise to include at least a couple of "walks on water" written references. Some applicants simply write "references available upon request" at the bottom of their résumés. To me, this shows total ignorance of the way search committees and often library administrators function. Every search committee operates under somewhat different rules, but if you are a member of the group making the first cut for telephone interviews, you are working your way though a large pile of paperwork. Since there's not a lot riding on a telephone interview, you don't need complete information on the applicants, but you do need something that sets them apart from the pack. A few written references may be all that's needed to place a name on the "A" list. If you are given nothing but names and contact information, you're going to have to do a little more work—probably calling a couple of references. If you have no contact information, your job is much harder. You must first call the applicant. Then the applicant must give you or send you the contact information, and then you must call some of the references. That's a lot of work to expend on one applicant at such an early stage. If all other factors are equal, you may decide it's not worth the effort. You have plenty of applications, and you can probably find enough qualified applicants without going to this additional effort.

At last, all your bits and pieces are winging their way (either virtually or physically) to their destination. It's time to move on to the next job opening and the next application package. This is not the time to make any assumptions about whether you will or will not be selected for this job. Nor is it the time to agonize over what you might have written. Keep your cover letter and résumé easily available in case you get a phone call out of the blue, but don't allow yourself to become discouraged by rejection letters (or postcards or nothing at all). Successful job hunters know from experience that they have a difficult road ahead and that sustained effort is the key to success.

RESOURCES

Crosby, O., et al. "Résumés, Applications, and Cover Letters." *Occupational Outlook Quarterly* 53, no. 2 (Summer 2009), 18–29.

Dessert, P. E. "Writing a Hot Résumé for Today's Job Market: A Tale of Two Engineers." *Manufacturing Engineering* 143, no. 5 (November 2009), 102–3.

Schaffer, G. "Six Ways to Ruin Your Résumé." *Computerworld* (Framingham, MA.) 43, no. 14 (April 13 2009), 26, 28.

Udechukwu, I., et al. "Job Applicants' Perceptions of Résumés versus Employment Application Forms in the Recruitment Process in a Public Organization." *Public Personnel Management* 38, no. 4 (Winter 2009), 79–96.

9

SURVIVING AND TRIUMPHING
SECRETS OF SUCCESSFUL INTERVIEWS

Over the course of your career, you have probably participated in a dozen or more job interviews. You may have carefully prepared before each one and even followed the tips provided in the many books on the subject. Much of this professional advice is still useful to you, but there are some additional hurdles you should know about. This chapter examines a number of typical interview situations and suggests some ways to approach them. If you are applying for a job close to home, the only telephone call you receive may be the one setting up a date and time for a face-to-face-interview. However, for nearly all out-of-town applications, a preliminary telephone interview with either a library administrator or search committee precedes the actual face-to-face interview. Since telephone interviews can pose special problems, let's begin there.

PREPARING FOR TELEPHONE INTERVIEWS

I've always wondered whether libraries conduct more telephone interviews than other employers. It's easy for libraries to advertise their positions regionally and nationally, so many applicants, especially for professional positions, are from out-of-state. In the past, libraries might have travel funds for perhaps two or three out-of-state interviews. Typically, they might first select a larger number of semifinalists for telephone interviews and then choose finalists from among that group. With budgets slashed, libraries are relying more on telephone interviews than ever before, so you'd better be prepared.

Unexpected Calls

We might begin by classifying telephone interviews into categories. First, they can be divided into scheduled and "out of the blue." An out-of-the-blue interview occurs when a library director or other administrator calls you to set up a time for a phone call. You start out trying to identify a time when you are both free and before you know it, you are describing your philosophy of library service. The caller may begin with a question or two about your qualifications or they may be calling to get a quick sense of what you're like. Some employers mistakenly imagine that if they can just talk with you for a few minutes, they will know instinctively whether you're worth pursuing.

This is a situation that you need to be prepared for, but more often, that initial call will come from an administrative assistant, search committee member, or library administrator who has other things to do with her time. They usually discuss only logistical issues, so you're off the hook (no pun intended) until the scheduled telephone interview.

Kinds of Calls

While I'm in classification mode, I think I would next divide telephone interviews into single interviewer calls, conference calls, and speaker phone ordeals. If you will just be talking with a library director or a department head, you will have a relatively easy time of it. Conference call technology has improved rapidly, and costs have diminished to the point that in many cases, such calls are free. A conference call allows all participants in the interview to have their own telephones and speak clearly into their receivers. However, search committees tend to get together with one another, conduct some committee business, and then call applicants while they are sitting at a desk or table with the speaker phone positioned somewhere near the middle. Again, audio technology has improved rapidly, and some high-quality microphones do a good job of picking up voices from both near and far. However, search committees often make their calls on whatever telephone happens to be available. This is what I call the speaker phone ordeal.

Preliminary Preparations

How will you deal with these multiple interview variations? Since libraries conduct more telephone interviews than face-to-face interviews, it stands to reason that you will be a participant in quite a few. You're going to need a plan to deal with both the expected and the unexpected call. Begin by making sure your answering machine or voice mail message communicates the right image. Ideally, you will want to use your landline for interviews because cell phones can be so problematic. However, you may share your landline with other family members. Work out an understanding with them that for the present, yours will be the voice that callers hear. That voice should be pleasant and professional with no jokes, music, or background noise. If you put more than one phone number on your résumé, be sure that callers get the same message. Now is a good time to make sure you have those premium services your phone company can provide. Caller ID is especially important, and if you're expecting a call from a prospective employer, call waiting and call forwarding can both be godsends.

Take a moment to consider how you answer your phone. Have telemarketers added a slightly suspicious note to your voice? I'm sometimes in the position of calling job applicants and have encountered decidedly unfriendly voices that, of course, become warm and friendly when they discover who I am. It's tough to forget that first impression. Your "unwelcome caller" voice is not the one you want a potential employer to hear. For the duration of your job hunt, answer each phone call in a warm, well-modulated tone of voice. You'll probably brighten the day of some surprised telemarketers.

Expecting the Unexpected

Then what? You'll make a better impression if you're familiar with the caller's name, so periodically go over the applications awaiting responses. In fact, if you've done your research, you will be familiar with a number of staff names. Even if it is a somewhat inconvenient time, try to appear happy that they called. If you really must go, let the caller know how much you'd like to talk with them, and ask to call them back later. Find a mutually agreeable time and make an effort to be the one who initiates the call. It is not unusual for administrative assistants or search committee members to forget to call back, especially if there are a number of interviews scheduled.

If the call is unexpected, you may be caught off guard, especially if you have submitted a large number of applications to various libraries. You're going to need some kind of cheat sheet close to the telephone. This could be a brief list of the jobs you've applied for, the libraries, the contact persons, and perhaps just a bit more information to jog your memory. If you can get to your computer, do so but sit down as soon as possible. Ideally, you need a comfortable chair and a solid surface to write on. Relax!

Gathering Information

If you're unprepared for the call, let the other person do most of the talking. At this point, you're most interested in collecting relevant information. Respond calmly but with enthusiasm. It might help to have a list of questions ready. It's almost inevitable that you will feel flustered and your mind will be racing, but this call is an important opportunity. You will want to know the date and time of the proposed telephone interview (Whose time zone, yours or theirs?), anticipated length of the interview, and names of the people you will be talking to. Although it's always possible to call back later, this golden opportunity should not be wasted. Use your best judgment about whether to extend the conversation. You're not prepared, so this may not be a good time to ask about the job itself.

Communicating with Groups

In general, telephone interviews with a committee are more difficult than with one individual. They require more preparation if you are to really communicate with each and every committee member. By the time of the scheduled call, you will need to have assembled as much information as possible about the library, the community in which the library is located, and the people who will be making the call. Make sure it's all written down so you can review it just before the call. You will inevitably be asked why you're interested in the position and your answer should focus on the positive information you have gathered, not on your financial desperation. Be sure you've made a list of other generic interview questions that search committees frequently ask. Whenever possible, remember that your audience is more interested in their own world, not yours. Each time you take part in a telephone interview, spend a little time afterward jotting down the questions asked and add them to your list. However, each library is different so you can't depend entirely on a list of answers that was created for another library. Your responses should focus on this job, this library, and these individuals.

Predictable Questions

Remember that yours will be one of several telephone interviews, and all the other applicants will share the same playing field. In some ways, telephone interviews are more predictable than on-site ones because there tends to be less unscripted conversation. Committee members usually have a list of questions and they're taking notes on anything you say that's a little unexpected or different from the other applicants. Because interviews are more predictable, you can more effectively anticipate questions and problems.

Controlling Your Environment

Librarians I've talked with usually find speaker phone interviews the most stressful because it's so difficult to hear everyone. Laughter or paper shuffling can completely muffle the comments of the participants farthest from the microphone. However, all telephone interviews tend to be stressful. You might want to use the following suggestions to prepare for the call:

- Plan to be at home for the call. You can speak more freely and can better control your environment. Choose a time when other household members and barking dogs are out of the way.
- Select a desk or table and a comfortable chair. If you are comfortable consulting your computer screen during the interview, get it ready.
- Place your phone solidly on the table and make sure the cord is not tangled. If your phone is a cordless, be certain it is fully charged and set up near the base unit. Avoid using a cell phone and risking a dropped call.
- Clear your desk of everything that does not concern the interview. You will want to have your research close at hand, and you don't want to be scrambling through papers.
- Make sure you have a few pens for taking notes (ballpoints are notorious for running out of ink at critical moments).
- Make sure you have a glass of water for dry mouth and throat lozenges in case your voice gets froggy.

When the Phone Rings

Once you've exchanged pleasantries with some disembodied voices, your biggest challenge will be to establish a relationship with each of the people sitting in that distant office. Pay close attention when each committee member is introduced, repeat the name, and find it on your list. It's a good idea to make a comment or ask a question of each person as they are introduced. This is an effective way to get their attention, especially if you're their third interview of the day and they're feeling glazed and tired. We all want to be noticed and treated as individuals. If the chair rapidly lists the names of committee members, it's a good idea to interrupt the flow. He is reading from a prepared speech, and you've got to keep this from becoming a perfunctory "going through the motions" exercise. Explain that you want to be sure you heard correctly, then repeat the names and ask questions as above. You might also have other questions prepared for committee members that you can insert into the conversation later to revitalize the discussion when it seems to be dragging. Again, you want this to be an interesting conversation, not a required exercise.

You Can't Hear

If you're dealing with a speaker phone, you're going to miss some of the comments. It is always difficult to know whether you should ask members to repeat. Some repetition is necessary or you'll feel like you're talking to yourself. Too much of it can totally destroy the conversation's momentum. If you've done your homework, much of what they say will already be known to you. You can fit the words you do hear into what you already know, thus filling in some of the gaps. You may find yourself doing more of the talking because you know they can hear you but you can't hear them. However, avoid anything resembling a monologue, and don't allow technical problems to alter your strategy.

THE FACE-TO-FACE INTERVIEW

From a pool of, say, ten telephone interviews, the committee may choose three applicants to invite for face-to-face interviews. If the library is not paying travel expenses, the number may be larger. If you learn that you are among this select group, your odds have greatly improved. Now you have an opportunity to present yourself in the most positive light and demonstrate why and how you're the best person for the job.

Preparation Is Key

However, acing an interview takes a huge amount of preparation. If most of us were to walk into an interview right this moment, without any preplanning, we might be able to convince an interviewer that we are pleasant, even likeable, but we probably couldn't convince anyone that we are the best-qualified applicant for a job. It is essential to decide in advance what your most marketable assets are and package them for the interview. Identify your weaknesses too so you'll be prepared if they come up. You'll want to be honest, admit a weakness, and move on quickly to more positive discussion. Next, decide how you'll communicate important information without talking too much or coming across as a blowhard, all the while establishing a warm rapport with your interviewers. This is not an easy job, I'll grant you, but advance planning is half the battle.

The Perfect Applicant

Do you remember when Cinderella's fairy godmother waved her magic wand and transformed Cinderella into the perfect princess? You might want to think about what would be needed to transform you into the absolutely perfect applicant for the job you're seeking. Of course, it really would require a fairy godmother to change you into something you're not. However, it's probable that with a little spiffing up, you really can become a model applicant.

For this exercise, I'll pull out my imaginary magic wand and pop you into an interview with the director of a library. Of course, in real life, a long and bumpy road leads up to the interview. Many experienced job hunters warn that everything that can go wrong, will go wrong. When you're under stress and so much is riding on this one meeting, you tend to forget things and make stupid mistakes. It is, therefore, important to anticipate these issues and prepare for them. For example, your alarm clock doesn't go off, you underestimate the time it takes to drive to the library, or you make a wrong turn on a route you've traveled dozens of times. Give yourself some extra time, find a parking space, and then relax until it's time for the interview. Have a cup of coffee or go over your notes. No, perhaps no coffee. You might spill it on your carefully selected interview outfit. When it's very important for something to go well, it seems as if our "evil twins" try to defeat us at every turn, causing us to lose the address, misread the time and date of the interview, or forget our list of points to remember. Anticipate your evil twin's machinations and don't let him get the better of you.

First Impressions

For the moment, however, imagine that I've whisked you to the right office on the right floor on the right day. You walk into the office, shake hands, exchange pleasantries, and sit down. Let's assume that you are a 50-year-old experienced applicant (later I'll magically transform you into a recent LIS graduate to add a few more complications). It can be a challenge to rise gracefully from a squashy lounge chair without being a little clumsy. If you're given a choice, select the harder, firmer chair. Don't make an issue of it. Now is not the time to mention your arthritis or bad back.

Looking the Part

The library director is looking you over, making some snap judgments just as all of us would do in this situation. Having been in this situation before, I'm aware that library directors are just a little schizophrenic. On the one hand, we talk about wanting new blood in the library; we want youth and enthusiasm and a new staff member who doesn't bring stodgy old ideas. On the other hand, library directors tend to be in their 50s or 60s. They don't think of themselves as old or stodgy, so an older applicant may have a better chance than they might imagine. If I really did have a magic wand, I would give it a flick and make you five to ten years younger than the person interviewing you. Since I can't do that, you're going to have to work a little magic yourself. Most healthy people can look up to ten years younger than their chronological age and on a bad day they may look ten years older. Be sure this is one of your better days and spend some time making yourself look good for the interview.

Extra pounds may add extra years so be careful about your weight. Being unemployed is extremely stressful and when you feel stressed, you may tend to eat. Many people today are not only weight-conscious, but weight-obsessed. Prejudice against people who are overweight is common, and library administrators may make negative assumptions based on weight. Successful job applicants must radiate energy and enthusiasm. They must impress interviewers with their vitality and make it clear that they have plenty of stamina to devote to the new job.

Dress for Success

Don't go overboard, but spend a little time experimenting with a new look. You might want to try a new hair color or a change in makeup. Certainly, you will want to wear recently purchased, somewhat stylish clothing to the interview. I remember years ago gossiping with my colleagues about our humorous and not so humorous experiences with job interviews. Several of us admitted that we kept an interview outfit in the back of the closet. It was dressier than what we usually wore to work so it remained untouched, ever available in case we should want to apply for another job. I wonder how many years those interview outfits hung in the back of those closets before they were finally sent to Goodwill. If you own such an antique, it's time to do some shopping.

One reason we kept those perennial interview outfits ever available may have been that we were not quite sure what we should wear to an interview. Male librarians simply don't wear three-piece suits, and females don't usually wear four-inch heels. Images of model job applicants that we see in career articles may not feel right to us. Librarians vary widely in their clothing preferences. Some are very fashionable and others are just as frumpy as the stereotype portrays us. It is actually a lot easier to list the things you should not wear to an interview than what you should. For example:

- Avoid extremes that may attractive negative attention.
- Limit bright colors to accents and accessories.
- Avoid too tight outfits, short skirts, and plunging necklines.

Consider your environment. People tend to dress up more in urban areas and go for casual in small towns and suburbs. In my own Wyoming, suits and high heels seem ridiculous (we joke that black jeans constitute formal attire).

Bear in mind that librarians tend to be overly sensitive about their dowdy stereotype. At least in theory, most library administrators are looking for someone who looks hip and trendy. The only problem is that their idea of hip is probably quite different from that of a Madison Avenue executive. Discovering a happy medium is your challenge. A search committee may be harder to please than a single library administrator since they vary in age and interests.

The Captive Interviewer

As a librarian, you're accustomed to turning to books for enlightenment. You're used to helping your patrons satisfy their information needs, and when you yourself have such a need you know where to go. There are dozens of books about how to get a job, and you know better than anyone how to select the best of the lot. Build a small library and spend time at websites like ALA's JobLIST that are crammed with good ideas. In this book, I feel obligated to emphasize ways in which library jobs may be a little different from other kinds of jobs and librarians themselves are different.

For example, when I talk with librarians who frequently interview job applicants, neatness seems to be unusually high on their list. Of course, I don't regularly talk with post office supervisors or university deans or office managers about the subject, so I may be ill informed. However, a surprising number of library interviewers comment on dirty fingernails. Missing buttons on shirts and blouses seems to be another fixation. Aroma is the source of even more criticism (of course, body odor is a huge turnoff, but I've heard negative comments on relatively inoffensive perfumes).

Interviewers find themselves glued to a chair and closeted with a stranger for half an hour or more. They're trying to pay attention and ask the right questions, but this is not their favorite task and their attention tends to wander. They have little to look at except the applicant. Because sensory stimuli are limited, they become more aware of what they see and smell and hear. They don't mean to be nitpickers, but superficial defects that would normally go unnoticed take on more importance.

FROM THE INTERVIEWER'S CHAIR

I was recently talking with a new acquaintance who had just landed an especially desirable job. Since I was collecting information for this book, I practically cross-examined him on his secrets for success. Jim (not his real name) said that it definitely wasn't luck. He had been unemployed for several months and advanced to the interview phase several times, but had never gotten a job offer. Somehow he was doing something wrong, he reasoned, and since he'd been called for several interviews, the problem was probably not with his cover letter or résumé. He was doing something wrong during the interviews, or at least he was failing to say whatever magic words the interviewers were looking for.

In a flash of insight, Jim decided he was going at the problem from the wrong angle. Just as he'd been reading numerous books and articles about job hunting, it was reasonable to assume that library directors had done a fair amount of reading about interviewing techniques. Looking back, he realized there was a sameness about his interviews. There were some questions interviewers almost always asked but they didn't seem interested in his replies. Their eyes glazed and they appeared to be thinking about their grocery lists. It was as if these questions had been asked and answered so many times that they had become part of a meaningless ritual. For example, the applicant who isn't asked why he is interested in the job is rare indeed.

The Interesting Applicant

Not all his responses, however, were greeted with yawns. Interviewers seemed to listen intently to some of his responses. Searching library and business journals, it was not difficult to find articles containing interview tips for employers. In fact, it was as if he'd stumbled on trade secrets for choosing job applicants. Here are some of his discoveries:

Past performance can often predict future success. Thus, personnel experts recommend that applicants be asked to describe problems they encountered in the past and how they solved them. Such questions encourage applicants to reveal a lot, sometimes unconsciously, about themselves.

Employers, however, are much more interested in their own libraries and tend to create problem questions based on their own experience, not the applicant's. As we all know from Dale Carnegie, we are far more interested in ourselves and our own problems than in those of other people.

Actual interview questions, therefore, tend to be a combination of "Tell us about you" and "Tell us about ourselves." You can readily imagine which responses interviewers tend to remember.

It's Not about You

Jim made a list of all the questions he remembered being asked at past interviews. Then he listed additional questions recommended by personnel experts. It turned out that the list was not extremely long because interview questions are fairly predictable. Then he began crafting responses to each of the questions, keeping in mind that his responses must achieve two goals. He must provide enough information about himself to make it clear that he was well qualified for the position, but he must continually rekindle the attention of his audience by focusing on them and their library. He went over the questions again and again until he was sure he could answer the questions without hesitation, avoid common pitfalls, and present himself as an ideal choice for the position.

Looking back, Jim remembered that he had often done most of the talking. A bad sign, he decided. Listening is as useful a skill as talking. Of course, a potential employer wants to know about your experience but not at interminable length. What she really wants to know is whether you'll fit into the library. Unless you ask good questions and listen carefully to the answers, you won't know what she's looking for. You'll be making assumptions about what you think she wants, and you may be totally off the mark.

Online Detective Work

If you've really done your homework, you will know something about the people who will be interviewing you. Naturally, you exchange phone calls and/or e-mails with the person who's coordinating the search or sometimes with an administrative assistant. You will want to ask a variety of questions, and there is no reason not to inquire about who you will be meeting with. Once you have some names (and perhaps some other names you discover on the library's website), you can begin your research. Librarians are generally very visible on the Internet. You can often find them through journal articles, conference presentations, internal library reports, and even the minutes of committee meetings. You'll probably discover much that is familiar to you, but every library has its own personality and each is facing unique problems. The staff members you have identified are deeply involved in their world, and your challenge is to convince them that you share their concerns, understand their points of view, and would be a useful ally in helping them achieve their goals.

Fitting In

Librarians just entering the profession will need to convince employers that they have sufficient talent and experience to be successful. Your selling points are youth, enthusiasm, vitality, up-to-date skills, and openness to new ideas, but you'll also want to show that you possess enough maturity to hold your own. In the case of older librarians, experience and maturity are usually self-evident, but you must also demonstrate some of those youthful strengths like a willingness to embrace change, learn new skills, and fit comfortably into a new organizational structure. Your goal is not so much to tell the prospective employer how wonderful you are as how well you will fit into the new environment. Remember that most people try to hire other people who are like themselves. This, of course, means minimizing differences where possible and making it clear that you share the same values, priorities, and interests.

Just as it is necessary to sculpt your résumé into a slimmer, more manageable form, so too you will want to sculpt your responses at the interview. Which of your skills, courses, and work experiences are directly relevant to this job? Which can be made to sound as if they might be steps on a career ladder that leads to this particular position? Choose just a few. Carefully pick out the points you want to get across. If you don't know exactly what the job involves, you might want to hold an experience or two in reserve, but don't give in to the temptation to show off during the interview. Never do more than half the talking and don't allow yourself to go off into long stories. Each response should concisely answer a question, present you in a positive light, and personally involve your listeners. You may need to include some information without being asked, but keep these contributions to the essentials. If the library director or search committee have been interviewing other applicants, they're tired. At all costs, avoid being a bore.

Projecting Confidence

The best way to go into an interview is with the firm conviction that you are far and away the ideal applicant for the position. If you can really project conviction without appearing over-confident, there's a good chance that you can land the job. Because of the economy, you may find yourself applying for jobs that wouldn't normally interest you. Remember that you are not too good for the job, you are just right. You are neither overqualified nor underqualified. You are just right. It is a great opportunity for both you and the library. You are both lucky to have found one another and great things will come out of the relationship. Such upbeat, positive thoughts should be clear from your enthusiasm and relaxed self-confidence. While quiet confidence will score points, opinionated overconfidence is not attractive. You don't have all the answers, you don't fully understand the issues these librarians are dealing with, and once again, it's all about them, not you.

We all like to be liked. This sounds so simplistic, but achieving instant rapport with your interviewers can be the single most important part of the experience. By subtly making it clear to the interviewers that you are delighted to find such intelligent and congenial people, you can considerably improve your chances. When you're stressed and nervous, you may not find the interviewer delightful company and you may not be thinking about camaraderie or friendship. The more pleasant you make the experience for the interviewers, however, the more enthusiastically they are likely to look on your application.

Almost Enjoyable Interviews

Take a moment to consider how your interviewer is feeling. Not many people enjoy the job of interviewing job hopefuls. If you've ever done it yourself, you know that there can be only one applicant who gets the job and so the others will be disappointed. As caring human beings, we feel guilty at having to disappoint the majority of the people we interview. Keep the level of tension as low as possible, and don't press the interviewer about your chances for getting the job. Don't appear desperate or pathetic because that increases the strain on the interviewer. Most of us are essentially nice people, and we don't like hurting anyone. Don't beg and don't tell the interviewer what he or she should do.

It's important that the interviewer enjoy the interview. Don't forget to smile frequently and add a touch of humor when appropriate. Make a little fun of yourself, and have some very brief stories or comments ready that are specifically intended to entertain. One of the things that makes an interview different from a conversation with friends is that it must include a certain amount of what in any other circumstances would be bragging. Use humor to make it clear that you don't have a swelled head. If you've had a good interview, you can usually look back and recall moments when both you and the interviewers were laughing comfortably together. That's a pretty good indicator of success, but be careful of jokes about the interviewers or their library. You're an outsider and could easily stumble on a sensitive issue. Making fun of political figures or current controversies can also be dangerous. Making fun of yourself, however, shows that you're comfortable in your own skin and you don't take yourself too seriously.

Different Expectations

If you're interviewing with a larger library, you may have multiple interviews so a lot of people can meet you. Whether you have been invited for an extended visit or a single interview, canned questions tend to be very predictable. As I mentioned, many books and magazine articles list common ones, and you can add to the list by just looking back on your own experience. Different groups may have somewhat different questions. For example, faculty members would naturally like you to be interested in their disciplines, library paraprofessionals are looking for someone who views them with respect and whose company they will enjoy, local government administrators want to be sure you're a "regular fellow" and a team player. You might imagine yourself in different interviewers' chairs scanning your own résumé. A faculty member may be looking for advanced degrees and academic interests. An administrator is looking for skills that translate to the business world like supervisory and budgeting experience. What are the most negative questions it could suggest? How can you use those questions as springboards to present positive information about yourself?

Gaining Control of the Interview

Of course, you can't be all things to all people, and some must inevitably be disappointed. This brings up what I call the gentle art of redirection. Although you don't want to do all the talking in an interview, you do want to control it subtly. You may have only about half an hour to make an impression with each group. Sometimes it's more like fifteen minutes. A good upbeat half-hour, however, can be more effective than a long, weary afternoon. It means, however, that you're going to have to stay on message, as the media types put it. No matter what the interviewer's questions, you can almost always get across your positive qualities and qualifications. Examples allow you to demonstrate your innovative ideas and ability to solve problems. Practice ways to change the subject or revitalize the discussion if it seems it's slowing down.

Portfolios Can Redirect the Interview

Consider creating a portfolio that demonstrates your accomplishments and bringing it with you to the interview. Your portfolio could include a webpage design, pathfinders, brochures, and fliers. Just be sure that your portfolio is visually attractive (since interviewers can do little more than glance at it) and makes an instant, positive impression. Looking back, it seems to me that some interviews, through no fault of the applicants, lacked momentum. Perhaps it was late in the day and everyone was tired, or the search committee had been conducting interviews throughout the day. Portfolios may be most useful in such situations since they stop the interview in its tracks. Everyone looks at the portfolio materials, asks questions about them and how they were produced, and generally calls a time-out. If the interview has been generating energy and enthusiasm, this is not the time to change directions. On the other hand, applicants who don't have glitzy portfolios for show-and-tell purposes might consider some story or topic they can inject into the interview to revitalize the conversation. Recreational interests work well, and I have the impression that men have an appreciative audience if they display photos of a new baby or toddler. Unfortunately, this may not work for women since domestic topics can make them look less professional.

The Impression You Leave Behind

Be sure to end the interview on an upbeat note. Tell the group how much you've enjoyed talking with them (even if you have your fingers crossed behind your back). Encourage them to contact you if they have any other questions, and don't put too much emphasis on when and how you'll hear whether you got the job. Their last memory of you should be a positive one. Career counselors advise sending a thank-you note after the interview, just to keep that positive image fresh in their minds. I tend to prefer e-mail messages to individual members of the group because it's no longer natural to send snail-mail notes. The people you meet nearly always divulge their own personal interests or become especially interested in something about your past. Try to jot down notes about them and what seemed to interest them. It's hard to do this during the interview, so before you start your car for your journey home, take a few minutes to jot down whatever you remember about the people you met. Then when you send them e-mail messages thanking them for the interview, you can comment on something they said or expand on the topic that interested them. Interviewers may be acting as a group, but they are individuals who don't appreciate being lumped together.

It is inevitable that you will mentally replay the interview again and again. You will naturally be more likely to remember the gaffes you made than your more brilliant remarks. Nevertheless, if you did your homework, the interview probably progressed in much the same way as other interviews and you were well-prepared for many of its twists and turns. Of course, you said some less-than-brilliant things and true, you didn't realize you were walking into a landmine when you answered that politically charged question about collection development. Nevertheless, you did most things right. Of course, there are circumstances over which you have no control. With the job market in its current depressing state, you were probably up against a number of well-qualified applicants, and one may be a more perfect fit for this particular job. However, with each interview your technique will improve, and it will not be long before you join the ranks of the fully and I hope happily employed.

RESOURCES

Herreid, C. F., et al. "How to Survive an Academic Job Interview." *Journal of College Science Teaching* 39, no. 3 (January/February 2010), 10–15.

Keegan, E. "Let's Talk About it." *Architect* (Washington, D.C.) 98, no. 10 (October 2009), 27–8.

Tougaw, P. W. "Twenty Minutes to Impress: Keys to a Successful Interview." *Kappa Delta Pi Record* 45, no. 2 (Winter 2009), 84–7.

VanDuinkerken, W., et al. "Looking Like Everyone Else: Academic Portfolios for Librarians." *The Journal of Academic Librarianship* 36, no. 2 (March 2010), 166–72.

INDEX

A

academic librarians
  faculty status for, 5
  as independent contractors, 54
  prospects for future, 1, 3
  references from faculty, 31
  tailoring résumé to institutional culture, 71
  use of curriculum vitae, 67
accomplishments on résumés, 70, 73
action verbs, hazards of, 70–71
administrators, interviewing with, 92
advertisements for jobs, analysis of, 57–58
age discrimination, concerns about, 59, 69
American Library Association JobLIST site, 23, 88
analytical skills, usefulness of, 4
answering machine outgoing message, 82
appearance of applicant and first impressions, 86–87
application forms, completing, 77–78
applications
  application package, 59–61
  customizing to job ad, 60
  following instructions in, 60
  identifying the perfect applicant, 59, 86
  research on employer, 57–58
  See also cover letters; résumés
applications, e-mail, 79–80
applications, faxed, 79
applications, online, 78
archivists, job potential for, 3
attorney, consultation with, 30
automation and continuing need for professional positions, 5
awards kept in home office, 22

B

baby pictures, use of by male interviewees, 93
bibliographers, decline in need for, 10
bill payments, priorities for, 33
blogging, 44
boss, relationship with
  avoiding criticism of, 33
  and job security, 18
budget, personal. *See* financial matters
budget crisis in libraries
  effect on hiring, vii
  effect on staffing levels, 1–2
  estimating management's response to, 13
buttons, missing, on interviewees, 88

C

caller ID, use of, 82
career changing as option, 54–55
career patterns in résumé story, 67–68, 69
cataloging as disappearing job, 9–10, 16, 50
cell phones, unreliability of, 35, 82, 84
chairs, choice of, for interviews, 86
change in direction, planning for, 47–55
  changing job type/and disappearing jobs, 50–52
  relocation, 49–50
  and retirement, 53
  technology issues, 52
children's services as growing specialty, 9
clothing for interview, 87
COBRA benefits, 25, 32
commendations kept in home office, 22
communication skills expressed in cover letter, 63
community, research on, 58
computer equipment for job hunting, 36–37
computer skills. *See* technology skills
conference call interviews, 82
confidence, projecting, 91
"consultant," use of on résumé, 72
consulting after termination, 30–31
contacts
  information kept in home office, 22
  and recreational interests, 34
  uses of, 40, 45
  See also networking
copy editing of cover letters, 65
cordless phones, use of, 84
corporate environments. *See* special librarians
cost of living and decision to relocate, 49
counseling
  and coping with stress, 26
  for debt management, 32
cover letters
  in e-mail applications, 79
  layoffs in, 71
  length of, 61–62
  omission of negatives, 63
  and research on hiring decision makers, 58
curriculum vitae (CV), use of, 67
customized answers to interview questions, 83–84

D

database for information management, 37
dates on résumé
  and age of applicant, 69

dates on résumé (cont.)
    and appearance of job hopping, 73
    and gaps in employment, 71
debt management, 32
decision-making authority of professional job descriptions, 5
depression, coping with, 26, 33
desk for job hunting, 35
digital records, job potential for, 3
digital resources, effect on staffing needs, 3
digitization projects, restructuring of job descriptions for, 6
disappearing jobs, 50
downsizing of professional positions to paraprofessional level, 4, 5, 15–16
dressing for interview, 87

E

education and training on résumé, 73, 74
education in retirement, 54
electronic discussion lists, 23, 40
electronic records, job potential for, 3
e-mail accounts
    for job hunting, 40
    saving e-mails off site, 22–23
    using personal domain name, 45
e-mail applications, 79–80
e-mail messages
    after interviews, 93
    filing of, 36–37
emotional effect of unemployment
    and checklists of things to do, 21–24
    depression, 26, 33
    and personal relationships, 25–26
    and planning for layoffs, viii, 19
employers, research on, 41, 44, 57–58, 90
employment outlook, 3
enjoyment in interviewing, 91–92
enjoyment in job hunting, 65
enthusiasm in applicants, 59, 91
environment for telephone interviews, 84
exercise and coping with stress, 25
expenses, reducing, 24–25, 32
experience
    description of, 69, 72
    exaggeration of, 71
    See also résumés
experienced librarians
    first impressions of, 86
    omission of work history from cover letter, 63
    outdated skills on résumés, 74
    overcoming image of too old, 59, 69
    strengths of, 74, 87
    upgrading skills, 23–24, 51, 62, 73, 74
    use of personal contacts, 40
    See also second career librarians

F

face-to-face interviews, 85–88
faculty members, interviewing with, 92
family, effect on
    and coping with layoffs, 25–26
    and gaps in work experience, 73
    of relocation, 48–49
    on spouse's income, 32
faxed applications, 79
federal programs for unemployed, 30
filing system for job hunt, 36–37
financial matters
    and family, 26
    for job hunting, viii, 36, 50
    planning for layoffs, 24–25
    and stress, 24, 32
first impressions at interviews, 86
fitting in, in interviews, 90
flash drives, e-mail contact information on, 22–23
freelancing as retirement plan, 54
friends after loss of job, 34
    See also networking

G

gaps in résumé for family concerns, 73
goals and objectives of library and recession-proofing the job, 16
gossip about former job, avoidance of, 33
government documents librarians, decline in need for, 9–10, 50
grace periods on bill payments, 33
grammar and spelling, importance of, 61, 63–64
grieving the loss of the job, 33

H

happiness, effect of relocation on, 49
health care benefits, planning for, 25–26, 30, 32
hiring decision makers, researching, 58
hobbies and recreational interests
    and contact with other people, 34
    developed into small business, 54–55
    as experience on résumé, 72
    in interviews, 93
    as padding on résumé, 75
home businesses
    as experience on résumé, 72
    as option after layoff, 54–55
home office, 22, 32
home prices, effect on relocation, 48–49
housing expenses, priority of, 32
human resources director and layoffs, 30
humor
    in cover letter, 63
    in interviewing, 91–92

I

image of librarians, 4–5
independent contracting as retirement plan, 54
    See also "consultant," use of on résumé
information brokers, 3
insurance policies, cancellation of, 33
Internet access, 36
internships as experience on résumé, 72
interview outfits, choice of, 87
interview questions, preparation for, 82, 83, 89, 90
interviewers
    enjoyment of interview, 91–92
    establishing relationship with, 84–85, 91
    research on, 58, 90
    wandering attention in, 88–89
interviews
    face-to-face, 85–88
    management of, 90–93
    overcoming age prejudice in, 69
    recent course work as topic at, 73

telephone, 81–85
isolation, avoidance of, 34

J

job announcement quoted in cover letter, 62
job descriptions
    accuracy in, 14–15
    analysis of, 7
    including clerical tasks, 5
    out-of-date and job security, 17
job fairs, 40
job hopping, 69, 73
job hunting
    change of direction in, 47–55
    discovering job openings, 40–44
    evidence of for unemployment benefits, 32
    importance of starting immediately, 33
    narrowing, 38–39
    preparations for, 35–38
job ladder, invisible, 68
job loss, first aid for, 29–34
job postings, sources of, 23–24
job titles
    in cover letters, 62
    effect on image of librarians, 4–5
    invented titles, 69–70
    and job security, 17
    as measure of essentialness, 16
    for possible jobs, 39
    rebranding yourself for, 51
    titles which did not change when responsibilities changed, 69–70
    use of in résumé, 68, 69
    "volunteer," alternatives to, 72
JobLIST, 23, 41, 42, 88
jobsites, lists of, 41–42

L

late fees, avoidance of, 32
layoffs, planning for
    financial matters, 24–25
    self-care, 25–26
    strategies, 19, 21–24
legal rights in layoffs, 29–30
LibJobs electronic discussion list, 40
library, type of, for job hunt, 38–39
library association memberships, 23
library conferences
    networking at, 40
    speaking at, 45
library journals, print
    job listings in, 43–44
    writing for, 45
library schools
    alumni networks as source of information, 40
    effect on competition for library jobs, 49
    recent grads of (*See* recent grads)
    technology education in, 6–7
    upgrading skills at as planning for layoff, 23–24
LinkedIn social networking site, 23, 40
listening in interviews, 89
local job listings, sources of, 43
location for new job
    analysis of area, 48
    choice of, 38
    researching a distant location, 58
    and retirement plans, 54
longtime employees, 70

M

management as specialty, 7
mass mailing of applications, 65
materials selection, decline of jobs in, 15
maturity in recent grads, 90
moving, option of, 38
    See also location for new job

N

neatness as criterion for interviewees, 88
negative questions, preparation for, 92
negotiation of layoffs, 30
networking
    as advantage of part-time work, 31
    contact information kept at home, 22
    development of, 39–40, 45
    and job leads after layoff, 33
    and learning from other job seekers, 51
    LinkedIn social networking site, 23, 40
    for new grads, 5
    See also contacts, uses of
new grads. *See* recent grads
nontraditional librarian jobs
    exploration of, 51–52
    growth potential of, 3
    skills for, 4

O

office supplies for job hunt, 36
older applicants. *See* experienced librarians; second career librarians
online applications, 78
online discussion lists. *See* electronic discussion lists
online job sites, 40–41
organizational skills, usefulness of, 4
outsourcing, 5
overqualifications in education, 75
overweight people, prejudice against, 87

P

paraprofessional positions, accepting, 31, 39
part-time work
    after termination, 30–31
    and budget cuts, 2
    as option in retirement, 53–54
    See also consulting after termination
pay stubs and unemployment benefits, 32
PDF format for online applications, 79
perfumes on interviewees, 88
periodicals librarians, decline in need for, 9–10, 14–15
personal information in cover letters, 63
personality in cover letters, 63
personalization of cover letters, 64
personnel policy of library
    and job security, 18–19
    and layoffs, 30
pets and telephone interviews, 84
photocopied résumés, 76
placement centers at library conferences, 40, 41
placement centers at library schools, 51
portfolio in interview, 92–93
portfolios, uses of, 65, 92–93
printers, capabilities of, 36
prioritizing bill payments, 32
problem employees and need to cut staff, 14
problem solving
    as interview question, 89
    as job skill for new grads, 6

professional positions downgraded to paraprofessional, 4, 5, 15–16
proofreading the cover letter and résumé, 65, 76
psychological costs of job hunting, viii
public librarians, prospects for, 1, 3–4
public services librarians, 7
public speaking, 45

Q

quality of life issues and relocation, 50

R

rebranding yourself, 51
recent grads
    disadvantages of professionally designed résumés, 76
    interviewing for, 90
    nonprofessional experience on résumé, 69
    overcoming image of too young, 59
    problems facing, 5–7
    strengths of, 74
    use of job fairs, 40
    volunteer work or internships as experience on résumé, 72
recession-proofing a job, 13–14, 16–19
recessions, effect of, vii, 1–5
records management, job potential for, 3
recreational interests. *See* hobbies and recreational interests
reference, letters of
    in application packages, 80
    from colleagues and supervisors, 31, 33, 37–38
    from former boss, 33
    when forbidden by HR policy, 37–38
reference librarians and computer skills, 7
"references available upon request," 37, 79
regional job listings, 42–43
rejection letters, use of, 45–46, 80
relocating, option of, 38, 48–49
    See also visits to potential locations
research on employers, 44, 57–58, 90
résumé, length of, 76

résumé formats, 69–71, 75, 79
résumés, 67–80
    checklist for, 76–77
    concealing age in, 69
    expanded on in cover letter, 62
    other information on, 74–75
    professionally designed, 76
    for recent grads (*See* recent grads)
    for second career librarians, 10–11
    tailoring for different opportunities, 71, 76–77
    top section, importance of, 68, 70, 74
    updating and restructuring of, 22, 67–69
    on website, 44
résumés, annotated, 68, 70
résumés, topical, 74
retirement
    as method for cutting staff, 14
    as option after layoff, vii, 53–54
    restructuring of jobs after, 6
    as source of job vacancies, 2
retraining programs for unemployed, 30
return to job market on résumé, 73
rewards, use of, 37
rights of employees and job security, 18–19
routines, establishing, 37

S

savings, cashing in, 24
scanners, use of, 36, 78
school librarians, 2, 3–4, 23
screening of applications, surviving, 64, 77, 78–79
scripted interview questions, 84, 85
search engines and personal website, 45
second career librarians, advantages of, 10–11
self-employment
    as experience on résumé, 72
    as option after layoff, 54–55
self-worth, effect of job loss on, 45–46
seniority
    and essentialness of position, 16
    as method for cutting staff, 14
severance packages
    as incentive to retire, 2
    negotiation for, 30

skills, transferable, 73
smoking and coping with stress, 26
Social Security income, estimates of, 53
speaker phones in interviews, 82, 85
special librarians
    effect of recession on, 1
    as independent contractors, 3, 54
    job postings for, 23
    marketing by, 4
    references from clients, 31
specialties
    declining in importance, 9–10, 50–51
    targeting those gaining in popularity, 7–9
spending, moratorium on, 32
spouse and family. *See* family, effect on
stability in job on résumé/dates on, 69, 73
state job listings, 42–43
state programs for unemployed, 30
stationery for cover letters and résumés, 64–65, 76
staying on the job after termination, 30–31
strengths, focusing on, 74
stress, coping with
    and avoiding weight gain, 87
    and caring for yourself, 25
    and financial management, 24, 32
    and health, 26, 32, 87
    and health insurance, 32
    in interviews, 84, 86, 91
    and organization, 35, 37
    and part-time work, 30
    and personal relationships, 25–26
    and working after termination, 30–31
substitute librarians, working as, 31
supervisory skills
    and targeting management positions, 7
    for working with younger employees, 8
support groups, use of, 34, 39, 51
systems analysis, skills for, 4

T

tax revenues and employment of librarians, 2
tax withholding, adjustment of spouse's, 32
taxation of unemployment benefits, planning for, 32
technology skills
   as demonstrated on website, 44
   in job descriptions, 7
   and job security, 16–17
   and newer graduates, 6–7
   retraining programs, 30
   in second career librarians, 10–11
   upgrading of, 23, 51–52, 62, 73, 74
   usefulness of, 4
technology-related jobs, 8
telephone calls at inconvenient times, 83
telephone greeting, impressions from, 82
telephone interviews, 81–85
   arrangements for, 82, 83
   screening by and references, 80
   talking with a group, 82, 83
telephone services, 35
telephones
   cell phones, 35, 82, 84
   cordless phones, 84
   outgoing messages on, 82
   speaker phones, 82, 85
   in telephone interviews, 83, 84
temporary employee, working as after termination, 30–31
tenure and job security, 30
termination letter and unemployment benefits, 32
thank you notes after interviews, 93
to-do lists, use of, 22, 37
type font for cover letters and résumés, 64–65, 76
typewritten application forms, 78

U

unemployed, government programs for, 30
unemployment, periods of
   accounting for on résumé, 71
   preparing for, 21–24
unemployment benefits
   application for, 31–32
   and part-time work after termination, 31
   in planning for layoffs, 25
union memberships in layoffs, 18, 30

V

visits to potential locations, 50, 63
   See also relocating, option of
volunteer work as experience on résumé, 72

W

website, personal, 44
website hosting services, 45
work experience. *See* résumés
workspace, 35

Y

Yahoo's small business service, 45
young adult services as growing specialty, 9
younger applicants
   advantages of, 59
   and exaggeration of experience, 71
   See also recent grads

You may also be interested in

PRE- AND POST-RETIREMENT TIPS FOR LIBRARIANS
Edited by Carol Smallwood

A raft of veteran librarians, financial advisors, and other experts offer insight, inspiration, and tips for those already retired as well as those thinking about retiring.

ISBN: 978-0-8389-1120-4
176 PAGES / 6" X 9"

OTHER CAREER DEVELOPMENT TITLES

BE A GREAT BOSS
CATHERINE HAKALA-AUSPERK
ISBN: 978-0-8389-1068-9

WORKING IN THE VIRTUAL STACKS
EDITED BY
LAURA TOWNSEND KANE
ISBN: 978-0-8389-1103-7

HOW TO STAY AFLOAT IN THE ACADEMIC LIBRARY JOB POOL
EDITED BY TERESA Y. NEELY;
FOREWORD BY CAMILA A. ALIRE
ISBN: 978-0-8389-1080-1

ALSO BY JEANNETTE WOODWARD

COUNTDOWN TO A NEW LIBRARY, 2E
JEANNETTE WOODWARD
ISBN: 978-0-8389-1012-2

CREATING THE CUSTOMER-DRIVEN ACADEMIC LIBRARY
JEANNETTE WOODWARD
ISBN: 978-0-8389-0976-8

CREATING THE CUSTOMER-DRIVEN LIBRARY
JEANNETTE WOODWARD
ISBN: 978-0-8389-0888-4

Order today at **alastore.ala.org** or **866-746-7252!**
ALA Store purchases fund advocacy, awareness, and accreditation programs for library professionals worldwide.

www.ingramcontent.com/pod-product-compliance
Lightning Source LLC
Chambersburg PA
CBHW080808300426
44114CB00020B/2868